CAMBRIDGE LIBRARY COLLECTION

Books of enduring scholarly value

English Men of Letters

In the 1870s, Macmillan publishers began to issue a series of books called
'English Men of Letters' – biographies of English writers by other English
writers. The general editor of the series was the journalist, critic, politician,
and supporter (and later biographer) of Gladstone, John Morley (1838–
1923). The aim was to provide a short introduction to each subject and his
works, but also that the life should illuminate the works, and vice versa. The
subjects range chronologically from Chaucer to Thackeray and Dickens, and
an important feature of the series is that many of the authors (Henry James
on Hawthorne, Ward on Dickens) were discussing writers of the previous
generation, and some (Trollope on Thackeray) had even known their subjects
personally. The series exemplifies the British approach to literary biography
and criticism at the end of the nineteenth century, and also reveals which
authors were at that time regarded as canonical.

Wordsworth

The publication in 1798 of *Lyrical Ballads*, written by William Wordsworth
(1770–1850) and Samuel Taylor Coleridge, is considered to have launched
the Romantic movement. Published in 1881 in the first series of 'English Men
of Letters', this biography of Wordsworth by classical scholar and psychical
researcher F. W. H. Myers (1843–1901) shows how Wordsworth's profound
imagination and thought characterised and shaped his literary era. He
discusses the influence of Wordsworth's upbringing and love for the natural
world on works such as *The Excursion*, and *The Prelude*, which are said to
have marked the transition from neoclassicism to Romanticism. Showing
Wordsworth to be widely respected as 'so much besides a poet', Myers
describes the circumstances in which Wordsworth accepted the Laureateship
in 1843, an apparent surrender to 'the establishment' which poets such as
Robert Browning regarded as a betrayal of his own earlier radical idealism.

Cambridge University Press has long been a pioneer in the reissuing of out-of-print titles from its own backlist, producing digital reprints of books that are still sought after by scholars and students but could not be reprinted economically using traditional technology. The Cambridge Library Collection extends this activity to a wider range of books which are still of importance to researchers and professionals, either for the source material they contain, or as landmarks in the history of their academic discipline.

Drawing from the world-renowned collections in the Cambridge University Library, and guided by the advice of experts in each subject area, Cambridge University Press is using state-of-the-art scanning machines in its own Printing House to capture the content of each book selected for inclusion. The files are processed to give a consistently clear, crisp image, and the books finished to the high quality standard for which the Press is recognised around the world. The latest print-on-demand technology ensures that the books will remain available indefinitely, and that orders for single or multiple copies can quickly be supplied.

The Cambridge Library Collection will bring back to life books of enduring scholarly value (including out-of-copyright works originally issued by other publishers) across a wide range of disciplines in the humanities and social sciences and in science and technology.

Wordsworth

F.W.H. MYERS

CAMBRIDGE
UNIVERSITY PRESS

CAMBRIDGE UNIVERSITY PRESS

Cambridge, New York, Melbourne, Madrid, Cape Town,
Singapore, São Paolo, Delhi, Tokyo, Mexico City

Published in the United States of America by Cambridge University Press, New York

www.cambridge.org
Information on this title: www.cambridge.org/9781108034487

© in this compilation Cambridge University Press 2011

This edition first published 1881
This digitally printed version 2011

ISBN 978-1-108-03448-7 Paperback

English Men of Letters

EDITED BY JOHN MORLEY

WORDSWORTH

WORDSWORTH

BY

F. W. H. MYERS

"From worlds not quickened by the sun
A portion of the gift is won;
An intermingling of Heaven's pomp is spread
On ground which British shepherds tread."

London:

MACMILLAN AND CO.

1881.

CONTENTS.

WORDSWORTH.

WORDSWORTH.

CHAPTER I.

I CANNOT, perhaps, more fitly begin this short biography than with some words in which its subject has expressed his own feelings as to the spirit in which such a task should be approached. "Silence," says Wordsworth, "is a privilege of the grave, a right of the departed: let him, therefore, who infringes that right by speaking publicly of, for, or against, those who cannot speak for themselves, take heed that he opens not his mouth without a sufficient sanction. Only to philosophy enlightened by the affections does it belong justly to estimate the claims of the deceased on the one hand, and of the present age and future generations on the other, and to strike a balance between them. Such philosophy runs a risk of becoming extinct among us, if the coarse intrusions into the recesses, the gross breaches upon the sanctities, of domestic life, to which we have lately been more and more accustomed, are to be regarded as indications of a vigorous state of public feeling. The wise and good respect, as one of the noblest characteristics of Englishmen, that jealousy of familiar approach

B

which, while it contributes to the maintenance of private dignity, is one of the most efficacious guardians of rational public freedom."

In accordance with these views the poet entrusted to his nephew, the present Bishop of Lincoln, the task of composing memoirs of his life, in the just confidence that nothing would by such hands be given to the world which was inconsistent with the dignity either of the living or of the dead. From those memoirs the facts contained in the present work have been for the most part drawn. It has, however, been my fortune, through hereditary friendships, to have access to many manuscript letters and much oral tradition bearing upon the poet's private life;[1] and some details and some passages of letters hitherto unpublished, will appear in these pages. It would seem, however, that there is but little of public interest in Wordsworth's life which has not already been given to the world, and I have shrunk from narrating such minor personal incidents as he would himself have thought it needless to dwell upon. I have endeavoured, in short, to write as though the Subject of this biography were himself its Auditor, listening, indeed, from some region where all of truth is discerned and nothing but truth desired, but checking by his venerable presence any such revelation as public advantage does not call for, and private delicacy would condemn.

As regards the critical remarks which these pages contain, I have only to say that I have carefully consulted such notices of the poet as his personal friends have left

---

[1] I take this opportunity of thanking Mr. William Wordsworth, the son, and Mr. William Wordsworth, the grandson, of the poet, for help most valuable in enabling me to give a true impression of the poet's personality.

us, and also, I believe, nearly every criticism of importance which has appeared on his works. I find with
pleasure that a considerable agreement of opinion exists,—
though less among professed poets or critics, than among
men of eminence in other departments of thought or
action whose attention has been directed to Wordsworth's
poems. And although I have felt it right to express in
each case my own views with exactness, I have been able
to feel that I am not obtruding on the reader any merely
fanciful estimate in which better accredited judges would
refuse to concur.

Without further preface I now begin my story of
Wordsworth's life, in words which he himself dictated to
his intended biographer. "I was born," he said, "at
Cockermouth, in Cumberland, on April 7th, 1770, the
second son of John Wordsworth, attorney-at-law—as
lawyers of this class were then called—and law-agent to
Sir James Lowther, afterwards Earl of Lonsdale. My
mother was Anne, only daughter of William Cookson,
mercer, of Penrith, and of Dorothy, born Crackanthorp,
of the ancient family of that name, who from the times of
Edward the Third had lived in Newbiggen Hall, Westmoreland. My grandfather was the first of the name of
Wordsworth who came into Westmoreland, where he
purchased the small estate of Sockbridge. He was descended from a family who had been settled at Peniston, in
Yorkshire, near the sources of the Don, probably before
the Norman Conquest. Their names appear on different
occasions in all the transactions, personal and public, connected with that parish ; and I possess, through the kindness of Colonel Beaumont, an almery, made in 1525, at
the expense of a William Wordsworth, as is expressed in
a Latin inscription carved upon it, which carries the

pedigree of the family back four generations from himself. The time of my infancy and early boyhood was passed partly at Cockermouth, and partly with my mother's parents at Penrith, where my mother, in the year 1778, died of a decline, brought on by a cold, in consequence of being put, at a friend's house in London, in what used to be called ' a best bedroom.' My father never recovered his usual cheerfulness of mind after this loss, and died when I was in my fourteenth year, a schoolboy, just returned from Hawkshead, whither I had been sent with my elder brother Richard, in my ninth year.

"I remember my mother only in some few situations, one of which was her pinning a nosegay to my breast, when I was going to say the catechism in the church, as was customary before Easter. An intimate friend of hers told me that she once said to her, that the only one of her five children about whose future life she was anxious was William ; and he, she said, would be remarkable, either for good or for evil. The cause of this was, that I was of a stiff, moody, and violent temper ; so much so that I remember going once into the attics of my grandfather's house at Penrith, upon some indignity having been put upon me, with an intention of destroying myself with one of the foils, which I knew was kept there. I took the foil in hand, but my heart failed. Upon another occasion, while I was at my grandfather's house at Penrith, along with my eldest brother, Richard, we were whipping tops together in the large drawing-room, on which the carpet was only laid down upon particular occasions. The walls were hung round with family pictures, and I said to my brother, ' Dare you strike your whip through that old lady's petticoat?' He replied, 'No, I won't.' 'Then, said I, ' here goes ! ' and I struck my lash through her

hooped petticoat; for which, no doubt, though I have
forgotten it, I was properly punished. But, possibly
from some want of judgment in punishments inflicted, I
had become perverse and obstinate in defying chastisement,
and rather proud of it than otherwise.

"Of my earliest days at school I have little to say, but
that they were very happy ones, chiefly because I was
left at liberty then, and in the vacations, to read whatever
books I liked. For example, I read all Fielding's works,
Don Quixote, Gil Blas, and any part of Swift that I liked—
Gulliver's Travels, and the *Tale of the Tub,* being both
much to my taste. It may be, perhaps, as well to mention,
that the first verses which I wrote were a task imposed by
my master; the subject, *The Summer Vacation;* and of
my own accord I added others upon *Return to School.*
There was nothing remarkable in either poem; but I was
called upon, among other scholars, to write verses upon
the completion of the second centenary from the foundation of the school in 1585 by Archbishop Sandys. These
verses were much admired—far more than they deserved,
for they were but a tame imitation of Pope's versification,
and a little in his style."

But it was not from exercises of this kind that Wordsworth's school-days drew their inspiration. No years
of his life, perhaps, were richer in strong impressions;
but they were impressions derived neither from books nor
from companions, but from the majesty and loveliness of
the scenes around him;—from Nature, his life-long mistress,
loved with the first heats of youth. To her influence we
shall again recur; it will be most convenient first to trace
Wordsworth's progress through the curriculum of ordinary
education.

It was due to the liberality of Wordsworth's two

uncles, Richard Wordsworth and Christopher Crackanthorp (under whose care he and his brothers were placed
at their father's death, in 1783), that his education was
prolonged beyond his school-days. For Sir James Lowther, afterwards Lord Lonsdale,—whose agent Wordsworth's
father, Mr. John Wordsworth, was—becoming aware that
his agent had about 5000*l.* at the bank, and wishing,
partly on political grounds, to make his power over him
absolute, had forcibly borrowed this sum of him, and then
refused to repay it. After Mr. John Wordsworth's death
much of the remaining fortune which he left behind him
was wasted in efforts to compel Lord Lonsdale to refund
this sum ; but it was never recovered till his death in
1801, when his successor repaid 8500*l.* to the Wordsworths, being a full acquittal, with interest, of the original
debt. The fortunes of the Wordsworth family were, therefore, at a low ebb in 1787, and much credit is due to the
uncles who discerned the talents of William and Christopher, and bestowed a Cambridge education on the future
Poet Laureate, and the future Master of Trinity.

In October, 1787, then, Wordsworth went up as an
undergraduate to St. John's College, Cambridge. The
first court of this College, in the south-western corner of
which were Wordsworth's rooms, is divided only by a
narrow lane from the Chapel of Trinity College, and his
first memories are of the Trinity clock, telling the hours
" twice over, with a male and female voice," of the pealing
organ, and of the prospect when

> From my pillow looking forth, by light
> Of moon or favouring stars I could behold
> The antechapel, where the statue stood
> Of Newton with his prism and silent face,
> The marble index of a mind for ever
> Voyaging through strange seas of Thought, alone.

For the most part the recollections which Wordsworth brought away from Cambridge are such as had already found expression more than once in English literature ; for it has been the fortune of that ancient University to receive in her bosom most of that long line of poets who form the peculiar glory of our English speech. Spenser, Ben Jonson, and Marlowe ; Dryden, Cowley, and Waller; Milton, George Herbert, and Gray—to mention only the most familiar names—had owed allegiance to that mother who received Wordsworth now, and Coleridge and Byron immediately after him. " Not obvious, not obtrusive, she ;" but yet her sober dignity has often seemed no unworthy setting for minds, like Wordsworth's, meditative without languor, and energies advancing without shock or storm. Never, perhaps, has the spirit of Cambridge been more truly caught than in Milton's *Penseroso ;* for this poem obviously reflects the seat of learning which the poet had lately left, just as the *Allegro* depicts the cheerful rusticity of the Buckinghamshire village which was his new home. And thus the *Penseroso* was understood by Gray, who, in his *Installation Ode*, introduces Milton among the bards and sages who lean from heaven,

> To bless the place where, on their opening soul,
> First the genuine ardour stole.

" 'Twas Milton struck the deep-toned shell," and invoked with the old affection the scenes which witnessed his best and early years :

> Ye brown o'er-arching groves,
> That contemplation loves,
> Where willowy Camus lingers with delight !
> Oft at the blush of dawn

I trod your level lawn,
Oft wooed the gleam of Cynthia silver-bright
In cloisters dim, far from the haunts of Folly,
With Freedom by my side, and soft-eyed Melancholy.

And Wordsworth also "on the dry smooth-shaven green "
paced on solitary evenings " to the far-off curfew's sound,"
beneath those groves of forest-trees among which " Philo-
mel still deigns a song " and the spirit of contemplation
lingers still; whether the silent avenues stand in the
summer twilight filled with fragrance of the lime, or the
long rows of chestnut engirdle the autumn river-lawns
with walls of golden glow, or the tall elms cluster in
garden or *Wilderness* into towering citadels of green.
Beneath one exquisite ash-tree, wreathed with ivy, and
hung in autumn with yellow tassels from every spray,
Wordsworth used to linger long. " Scarcely Spenser's
self," he tells us,

Could have more tranquil visions in his youth,
Or could more bright appearances create
Of human forms with superhuman powers,
Than I beheld loitering on calm clear nights
Alone, beneath this fairy work of earth.

And there was another element in Wordsworth's life at
Cambridge more peculiarly his own—that exultation which
a boy born among the mountains may feel when he per-
ceives that the delight in the external world which the
mountains have taught him has not perished by uprooting,
nor waned for want of nourishment in field or fen ; that
even here, where nature is unadorned, and scenery, as it
were, reduced to its elements,—where the prospect is but
the plain surface of the earth, stretched wide beneath an
open heaven,— even here he can still feel the early glow,

can take delight in that broad and tranquil greenness, and in the august procession of the day.

> As if awakened, summoned, roused, constrained,
> I looked for universal things; perused
> The common countenance of earth and sky—
> Earth, nowhere unembellished by some trace
> Of that first Paradise whence man was driven ;
> And sky, whose beauty and bounty are expressed
> By the proud name she bears—the name of Heaven.

Nor is it only in these open air scenes that Wordsworth has added to the long tradition a memory of his own. The "storied windows richly dight," which have passed into a proverb in Milton's song, cast in King's College Chapel the same "soft chequerings" upon their framework of stone while Wordsworth watched through the pauses of the anthem the winter afternoon's departing glow :

> Martyr, or King, or sainted Eremite,
> Whoe'er ye be that thus, yourselves unseen,
> Imbue your prison-bars with solemn sheen,
> Shine on, until ye fade with coming Night.

From those shadowy seats whence Milton had heard " the pealing organ blow to the full-voiced choir below," Wordsworth too gazed upon—

> That branching roof
> Self-poised, and scooped into ten thousand cells
> Where light and shade repose, where music dwells
> Lingering, and wandering on as loth to die—
> Like thoughts whose very sweetness yieldeth proof
> That they were born for immortality.

Thus much, and more, there was of ennobling and unchangeable in the very aspect and structure of that ancient University, by which Wordsworth's mind was bent towards

a kindred greatness. But of active moral and intellectual
life there was at that time little to be found within her
walls. The floodtide of her new life had not yet set in;
she was still slumbering, as she had slumbered long, content to add to her majesty by the mere lapse of generations, and increment of her ancestral calm. Even had
the intellectual life of the place been more stirring, it is
doubtful how far Wordsworth would have been welcomed,
or deserved to be welcomed, by authorities or students.
He began residence at seventeen, and his northern nature
was late to flower. There seems, in fact, to have been
even less of visible promise about him than we should
have expected; but rather something untamed and in-
subordinate, something heady and self-confident; an independence that seemed only rusticity, and an indolent
ignorance which assumed too readily the tones of scorn.
He was as yet a creature of the lakes and mountains,
and love for Nature was only slowly leading him to love
and reverence for man. Nay, such attraction as he had
hitherto felt for the human race had been interwoven
with her influence in a way so strange that to many
minds it will seem a childish fancy not worth recounting.
The objects of his boyish idealization had been Cumbrian
shepherds—a race whose personality seems to melt into
Nature's—who are united as intimately with moor and
mountain as the petrel with the sea.

> A rambling schoolboy, thus
> I felt his presence in his own domain
> As of a lord and master—or a power,
> Or genius, under Nature, under God,
> Presiding; and severest solitude
> Had more commanding looks when he was there.
> When up the lonely brooks on rainy days
> Angling I went, or trod the trackless hills

By mists bewildered, suddenly mine eyes
Have glanced upon him distant a few steps,
In size a giant, stalking through thick fog,
His sheep like Greenland bears ; or, as he stepped
Beyond the boundary line of some hill-shadow,
His form hath flashed upon me, glorified
By the deep radiance of the setting sun ;
Or him have I descried in distant sky,
A solitary object and sublime,
Above all height ! like an aërial cross
Stationed alone upon a spiry rock
Of the Chartreuse, for worship. Thus was man
Ennobled outwardly before my sight ;
And thus my heart was early introduced
To an unconscious love and reverence
Of human nature ; hence the human form
To me became an index of delight,
Of grace and honour, power and worthiness.

"This sanctity of Nature given to man,"—this inter-
fusion of human interest with the sublimity of moor and
hill,—formed a typical introduction to the manner in which
Wordsworth regarded mankind to the end,—depicting him
as set, as it were, amid impersonal influences, which make
his passion and struggle but a little thing ; as when
painters give but a strip of their canvas to the fields and
cities of men, and overhang the narrowed landscape with
the space and serenity of heaven.

To this distant perception of man—of man "purified,
removed, and to a distance that was fit"—was added, in
his first summer vacation, a somewhat closer interest in the
small joys and sorrows of the villagers of Hawkshead,—a
new sympathy for the old Dame in whose house the poet
still lodged, for "the quiet woodman in the woods," and
even for the "frank-hearted maids of rocky Cumberland,"
with whom he now delighted to spend an occasional
evening in dancing and country mirth. And since the

events in this poet's life are for the most part inward and
unseen, and depend upon some shock and coincidence
between the operations of his spirit and the cosmorama
of the external world, he has recorded with especial em-
phasis a certain sunrise which met him as he walked
homewards from one of these scenes of rustic gaiety,—a
sunrise which may be said to have begun that poetic
career which a sunset was to close :

> Ah! need I say, dear Friend! that to the brim
> My heart was full ; I made no vows, but vows
> Were then made for me ; bond unknown to me
> Was given, that I should be, else sinning greatly,
> A dedicated Spirit.

His second long vacation brought him a further gain in
human affections. His sister, of whom he had seen little
for some years, was with him once more at Penrith, and
with her another maiden,

> By her exulting outside look of youth
> And placid under-countenance, first endeared ;

whose presence now laid the foundation of a love which
was to be renewed and perfected when his need for it was
full, and was to be his support and solace to his life's end.
His third long vacation he spent in a walking tour in
Switzerland. Of this, now the commonest relaxation of
studious youth, he speaks as of an " unprecedented course,"
indicating " a hardy slight of college studies and their
set rewards." And it seems, indeed, probable that
Wordsworth and his friend Jones were actually the
first undergraduates who ever spent their summer in
this way. The pages of the *Prelude* which narrate this
excursion, and especially the description of the crossing
of the Simplon,—

The immeasurable height
Of woods decaying, never to be decayed,—

form one of the most impressive parts of that singular
autobiographical poem, which, at first sight so tedious
and insipid, seems to gather force and meaning with each
fresh perusal. These pages, which carry up to the verge
of manhood the story of Wordsworth's career, contain,
perhaps, as strong and simple a picture as we shall anywhere find of hardy English youth,—its proud self-suf-
ficingness and careless independence of all human things.
Excitement, and thought, and joy, seem to come at once
at its bidding ; and the chequered and struggling existence
of adult men seems something which it need never enter,
and hardly deigns to comprehend.

Wordsworth and his friend encountered on this tour
many a stirring symbol of the expectancy that was running through the nations of Europe. They landed at
Calais " on the very eve of that great federal day " when
the Trees of Liberty were planted all over France. They
met on their return

The Brabant armies on the fret
For battle in the cause of liberty.

But the exulting pulse that ran through the poet's
veins could hardly yet pause to sympathize deeply even
with what in the world's life appealed most directly to
ardent youth.

A stripling, scarcely of the household then
Of social life, I looked upon these things
As from a distance ; heard, and saw, and felt —
Was touched, but with no intimate concern.
I seemed to move along them as a bird
Moves through the air—or as a fish pursues
Its sport, or feeds in its proper element.

I wanted not that joy, I did not need
Such help.   The ever-living universe,
Turn where I might, was opening out its glories ;
And the independent spirit of pure youth
Called forth at every season new delights,
Spread round my steps like sunshine o'er green fields.

CHAPTER II.

WORDSWORTH took his B.A. degree in January, 1791, and quitted Cambridge with no fixed intentions as to his future career. " He did not feel himself," he said long afterwards, " good enough for the Church ; he felt that his mind was not properly disciplined for that holy office, and that the struggle between his conscience and his impulses would have made life a torture. He also shrank from the law. He had studied military history with great interest, and the strategy of war ; and he always fancied that he had talents for command ; and he at one time thought of a military life ; but then he was without connexions, and he felt if he were ordered to the West Indies his talents would not save him from the yellow fever, and he gave that up." He therefore repaired to London, and lived there for a time on a small allowance and with no definite aim. His relations with the great city were of a very slight and external kind. He had few acquaintances, and spent his time mainly in rambling about the streets. His descriptions of this phase of his life have little interest. There is some flatness in an enumeration of the nationalities observable in a London crowd, concluding thus :—

> Malays, Lascars, the Tartar, the Chinese,
> And Negro Ladies in white muslin gowns.

But Wordsworth's limitations were inseparably connected with his strength. And just as the flat scenery of Cambridgeshire had only served to intensify his love for such elements of beauty and grandeur as still were present in sky and fen, even so the bewilderment of London taught him to recognize with an intenser joy such fragments of things rustic, such aspects of things eternal, as were to be found amidst that rush and roar. To the frailer spirit of Hartley Coleridge the weight of London might seem a load impossible to shake off. "And what hath Nature," he plaintively asked,—

> And what hath Nature but the blank void sky
> And the thronged river toiling to the main ?

But Wordsworth saw more than this. He became, as one may say, the poet not of London considered as London, but of London considered as a part of the country. Like his own *Farmer of Tilsbury Vale*—

> In the throng of the Town like a Stranger is he,
> Like one whose own Country's far over the sea ;
> And Nature, while through the great city he hies,
> Full ten times a day takes his heart by surprise.

Among the poems describing these sudden shocks of vision and memory none is more exquisite than the *Reverie of Poor Susan :*

> At the corner of Wood Street, when daylight appears,
> Hangs a Thrush that sings loud, it has sung for three years :
> Poor Susan has passed by the spot, and has heard
> In the silence of morning the song of the Bird.
>
> 'Tis a note of enchantment ; what ails her ? She sees
> A mountain ascending, a vision of trees ;
> Bright volumes of vapour through Lothbury glide,
> And a river flows on through the vale of Cheapside.

The picture is one of those which come home to many
a country heart with one of those sudden "revulsions
into the natural" which philosophers assert to be the
essence of human joy. But noblest and best known of
all these poems is the *Sonnet on Westminster Bridge*,
"Earth hath not anything to show more fair;" in which
nature has reasserted her dominion over the works of all
the multitude of men ; and in the early clearness the poet
beholds the great City—as Sterling imagined it on his
dying-bed—" not as full of noise and dust and confusion,
but as something silent, grand and everlasting." And
even in later life, when Wordsworth was often in London,
and was welcome in any society, he never lost this external manner of regarding it. He was always of the
same mind as the group of listeners in his *Power of
Music :*

> Now, Coaches and Chariots! roar on like a stream !
> Here are twenty Souls happy as souls in a dream :
> They are deaf to your murmurs, they care not for you,
> Nor what ye are flying, nor what ye pursue !

He never made the attempt,—vulgarized by so many a
"fashionable novelist," and in which no poet has succeeded yet,—to disentangle from that turmoil its elements
of romance and of greatness ; to enter that realm of
emotion where Nature's aspects become the scarcely noted
accessory of vicissitudes that transcend her own ; to trace
the passion or the anguish which whirl along some lurid
vista toward a sun that sets in storm, or gaze across silent
squares by summer moonlight amid a smell of dust and
flowers.

But although Wordsworth passed thus through London
unmodified and indifferent, the current of things was
sweeping him on to mingle in a fiercer tumult,—to be

c

caught in the tides of a more violent and feverish life.
In November 1791 he landed in France, meaning to pass
the winter at Orleans and learn French.   Up to this date
the French Revolution had impressed him in a rather
unusual manner,—namely, as being a matter of course.
The explanation of this view is a somewhat singular one.
Wordsworth's was an old family, and his connexions
were some of them wealthy and well placed in the world;
but the chances of his education had been such that he
could scarcely realize to himself any other than a democratic type of society.   Scarcely once, he tells us, in his
school days had he seen boy or man who claimed respect
on the score of wealth and blood; and the manly atmosphere of Cambridge preserved even in her lowest days a
society

> Where all stood thus far
> Upon equal ground; that we were brothers all
> In honour, as in one community,
> Scholars and gentlemen;

while the teachings of nature and the dignity of Cumbrian
peasant life had confirmed his high opinion of the essential worth of man.   The upheaval of the French people,
therefore, and the downfall of privilege, seemed to him no
portent for good or evil, but rather the tardy return of a
society to its stable equilibrium.   He passed through
revolutionized Paris with satisfaction and sympathy,
but with little active emotion, and proceeded first
to Orleans, and then to Blois, between which places he
spent nearly a year.   At Orleans he became intimately
acquainted with the nobly-born but republican general
Beaupuis, an inspiring example of all in the Revolution
that was self-devoted and chivalrous and had compassion
on the wretched poor.   In conversation with him Words-

worth learnt with what new force the well-worn
adages of the moralist fall from the lips of one who
is called upon to put them at once in action, and to
stake life itself on the verity of his maxims of honour.
The poet's heart burned within him as he listened.
He could not indeed help mourning sometimes at the
sight of a dismantled chapel, or peopling in imagination
the forest-glades in which they sat with the chivalry of a
bygone day. But he became increasingly absorbed in his
friend's ardour, and the Revolution—*mulier formosa
superne*—seemed to him big with all the hopes of man.

He returned to Paris in October 1792,—a month after
the massacres of September ; and he has described his
agitation and dismay at the sight of such world-wide
destinies swayed by the hands of such men. In a
passage which curiously illustrates that reasoned self-
confidence and deliberate boldness which for the most
part he showed only in the peaceful incidents of a literary
career, he has told us how he was on the point of putting
himself forward as a leader of the Girondist party, in the
conviction that his singleheartedness of aim would make
him, in spite of foreign birth and imperfect speech, a
point round which the confused instincts of the multitude
might not impossibly rally.

Such a course of action,—which, whatever its other
results, would undoubtedly have conducted him to the
guillotine with his political friends in May 1793,—was
rendered impossible by a somewhat undignified hindrance.
Wordsworth, while in his own eyes "a patriot of the
world," was in the eyes of others a young man of twenty-
two, travelling on a small allowance, and running his head
into unnecessary dangers. His funds were stopped, and
he reluctantly returned to England at the close of 1792.

And now to Wordsworth, as to many other English
patriots, there came, on a great scale, that form of sorrow
which in private life is one of the most agonizing of all—
when two beloved beings, each of them erring greatly,
become involved in bitter hate. The new-born Republic
flung down to Europe as her battle-gage the head of a
king. England, in an hour of horror that was almost panic,
accepted the defiance, and war was declared between the
two countries early in 1793. "No shock," says Wordsworth,

> Given to my moral nature had I known
> Down to that very moment; neither lapse
> Nor turn of sentiment that might be named
> A revolution, save at this one time;

and the sound of the evening gun-fire at Portsmouth
seemed at once the embodiment and the premonition of
England's guilt and woe.

Yet his distracted spirit could find no comfort in the
thought of France. For in France the worst came to the
worst; and everything vanished of liberty except the
crimes committed in her name.

> Most melancholy at that time, O Friend!
> Were my day-thoughts, my nights were miserable.
> Through months, through years, long after the last beat
> Of those atrocities, the hour of sleep
> To me came rarely charged with natural gifts—
> Such ghastly visions had I of despair,
> And tyranny, and implements of death; . . .
> And levity in dungeons, where the dust
> Was laid with tears. Then suddenly the scene
> Changed, and the unbroken dream entangled me
> In long orations, which I strove to plead
> Before unjust tribunals,—with a voice
> Labouring, a brain confounded, and a sense,
> Death-like, of treacherous desertion, felt
> In the last place of refuge—my own soul.

These years of perplexity and disappointment, following on a season of overstrained and violent hopes, were the sharpest trial through which Wordsworth ever passed. The course of affairs in France, indeed, was such as seemed by an irony of fate to drive the noblest and firmest hearts into the worst aberrations. For first of all in that Revolution, Reason had appeared as it were in visible shape, and hand in hand with Pity and Virtue; then, as the welfare of the oppressed peasantry began to be lost sight of amid the brawls of the factions of Paris, all that was attractive and enthusiastic in the great movement seemed to disappear, but yet Reason might still be thought to find a closer realization here than among scenes more serene and fair; and, lastly, Reason set in blood and tyranny and there was no more hope from France. But those who, like Wordsworth, had been taught by that great convulsion to disdain the fetters of sentiment and tradition and to look on Reason as supreme were not willing to relinquish their belief because violence had conquered her in one more battle. Rather they clung with the greater tenacity,—"adhered," in Wordsworth's words,

> More firmly to old tenets, and to prove
> Their temper, strained them more ;

cast off more decisively than ever the influences of tradition, and in their Utopian visions even wished to see the perfected race severed in its perfection from the memories of humanity, and from kinship with the struggling past.

Through a mood of this kind Wordsworth had to travel now. And his nature, formed for pervading attachments and steady memories, suffered grievously from the privation of much which even the coldest and calmest temper cannot forego without detriment and pain. For it is not with impunity that men commit themselves to the sole guidance of either of the two great elements of their being. The penalties of trusting to the emotions alone are notorious ; and every day affords some instance of a character that has degenerated into a bundle of impulses, of a will that has become caprice. But the consequences of making Reason our tyrant instead of our king are almost equally disastrous. There is so little which Reason, divested of all emotional or instinctive supports, is able to prove to our satisfaction that a sceptical aridity is likely to take possession of the soul. It was thus with Wordsworth ; he was driven to a perpetual questioning of all beliefs and analysis of all motives,—

> Till, demanding formal proof,
> And seeking it in everything, I lost
> All feeling of conviction ; and, in fine,
> Sick, wearied out with contrarieties,
> Yielded up moral questions in despair.

In this mood all those great generalized conceptions which are the food of our love, our reverence, our religion, dissolve away ; and Wordsworth tells us that at this time

> Even the visible universe
> Fell under the dominion of a taste
> Less spiritual, with microscopic view
> Was scanned, as I had scanned the moral world.

He looked on the operations of nature "in disconnection dull and spiritless ;" he could no longer apprehend her unity nor feel her charm. He retained indeed his craving for natural beauty, but in an uneasy and fastidious mood,—

> Giving way
> To a comparison of scene with scene,
> Bent overmuch on superficial things,
> Pampering myself with meagre novelties
> Of colour and proportion ; to the moods
> Of time and season, to the moral power,
> The affections, and the spirit of the place,
> Insensible.

Such cold fits are common to all religions : they haunt the artist, the philanthropist, the philosopher, the saint. Often they are due to some strain of egoism or ambition which has intermixed itself with the impersonal desire ; sometimes, as in Wordsworth's case, to the persistent tension of a mind which has been bent too ardently towards an ideal scarce possible to man. And in this case, when the objects of a man's habitual admiration are true and noble, they will ever be found to suggest some antidote to the fatigues of their pursuit. We shall see as we proceed how a deepening insight into the lives of the peasantry around him,—the happiness and virtue of simple Cumbrian homes,—restored to the poet a serener confidence in human nature, amid all the shame and downfall of such hopes in France. And that still profounder loss of delight in Nature herself,—that viewing of all things "in disconnection dull and spiritless," which, as it has been well said, is the truest definition of Atheism, inasmuch as a unity in the universe is the first element in our conception of God,—this dark pathway also was not without its outlet into the day. For the God in Nature is not only a God of Beauty, but a God of Law ; his unity can be apprehended in power as well as in glory ; and Wordsworth's mind, " sinking inward upon itself from thought to thought," found rest for the time in that austere religion,— Hebrew at once and scientific, common to a Newton and a

Job,—which is fostered by the prolonged contemplation of
the mere Order of the sum of things.

> Not in vain
> I had been taught to reverence a Power
> That is the visible quality and shape
> And image of right reason.

Not, indeed, in vain ! For he felt now that there is no
side of truth, however remote from human interests, no
aspect of the universe, however awful and impersonal,
which may not have power at some season to guide and
support the spirit of man. When Goodness is obscured,
when Beauty wearies, there are some souls which still
can cling and grapple to the conception of eternal Law.

Of such stern consolations the poet speaks as having
restored him in his hour of need. But he gratefully
acknowledges also another solace of a gentler kind. It was
about this time (1795) that Wordsworth was blessed with
the permanent companionship of his sister, to whom he
was tenderly attached, but whom, since childhood, he had
seen only at long intervals. Miss Wordsworth, after her
father's death, had lived mainly with her maternal grandfather, Mr. Cookson, at Penrith, occasionally at Halifax
with other relations, or at Forncett with her uncle Dr.
Cookson, Canon of Windsor. She was now able to join
her favourite brother ; and in this gifted woman Wordsworth found a gentler and sunnier likeness of himself ;
he found a love which never wearied, and a sympathy
fervid without blindness, whose suggestions lay so directly
in his mind's natural course that they seemed to spring
from the same individuality, and to form at once a portion
of his inmost being. The opening of this new era of
domestic happiness demands a separate chapter.

CHAPTER III.

MISS WORDSWORTH—LYRICAL BALLADS—SETTLEMENT AT GRASMERE.

FROM among many letters of Miss Wordsworth's to a beloved friend, (Miss Jane Pollard, afterwards Mrs. Marshall, of Hallsteads), which have been kindly placed at my disposal, I may without impropriety quote a few passages which illustrate the character and the affection of brother and sister alike. And first, in a letter (Forncett, February 1792), comparing her brothers Christopher and William, she says : " Christopher is steady and sincere in his attachments. William has both these virtues in an eminent degree, and a sort of violence of affection, if I may so term it, which demonstrates itself every moment of the day, when the objects of his affection are present with him, in a thousand almost imperceptible attentions to their wishes, in a sort of restless watchfulness which I know not how to describe, a tenderness that never sleeps, and at the same time such a delicacy of manner as I have observed in few men." And again (Forncett, June 1793), she writes to the same friend : "I have strolled into a neighbouring meadow, where I am enjoying the melody of birds, and the busy sounds of a fine summer's evening. But oh ! how imperfect is my pleasure whilst I am alone ! Why are you not seated with me ? and my dear William,

why is he not here also ?   I could almost fancy that I see
you both near me.   I hear *you* point out a spot, where if
we could erect a little cottage and call it our own we
should be the happiest of human beings.   I see my brother
fired with the idea of leading his sister to such a retreat.
Our parlour is in a moment furnished, our garden is
adorned by magic ; the roses and honeysuckles spring at
our command ; the wood behind the house lifts its head,
and furnishes us with a winter's shelter and a summer's
noonday shade.   My dear friend, I trust that ere long
you will be, without the aid of imagination, the companion of my walks, and my dear William may be of our
party. . . . He is now going upon a tour in the west of
England, with a gentleman who was formerly a schoolfellow,
—a man of fortune, who is to bear all the expenses of the
journey, and only requests the favour of William's company.   He is perfectly at liberty to quit this companion
as soon as anything more advantageous offers.   But it is
enough to say that I am likely to have the happiness of
introducing you to my beloved brother.   You must forgive me for talking so much of him ; my affection hurries
me on, and makes me forget that you cannot be so much
interested in the subject as I am.   You do not know him ;
you do not know how amiable he is.   Perhaps you reply,
' But I know how blinded you are.'   Well, my dearest,
I plead guilty at once ; I *must* be blind ; he cannot be so
pleasing as my fondness makes him.   I am willing to
allow that half the virtues with which I fancy him
endowed are the creation of my love ; but surely I may
be excused !   He was never tired of comforting his sister;
he never left her in anger ; he always met her with joy ;
he preferred her society to every other pleasure ;—or rather,
when we were so happy as to be within each other's reach,

he had no pleasure when we were compelled to be divided. Do not then expect too much from this brother of whom I have delighted so to talk to you. In the first place, you must be with him more than once before he will be perfectly easy in conversation. In the second place, his person is not in his favour—at least I should think not; but I soon ceased to discover this—nay, I almost thought that the opinion which I had formed was erroneous. He is, however, certainly rather plain; though otherwise has an extremely thoughtful countenance, but when he speaks it is often lighted up by a smile which I think very pleasing. But enough, he is my brother; why should I describe him? I shall be launching again into panegyric."

The brother's language to his sister is equally affectionate. "How much do I wish," he writes in 1793, "that each emotion of pleasure or pain that visits your heart should excite a similar pleasure or a similar pain within me, by that sympathy which will almost identify us when we have stolen to our little cottage. . . . I will write to my uncle, and tell him that I cannot think of going anywhere before I have been with you. Whatever answer he gives me, I certainly will make a point of once more mingling my transports with yours. Alas! my dear sister, how soon must this happiness expire; yet there are moments worth ages."

And again: in the same year he writes, "Oh, my dear, dear sister! with what transport shall I again meet you! with what rapture shall I again wear out the day in your sight! . . . I see you in a moment running, or rather flying, to my arms."

Wordsworth was in all things fortunate, but in nothing more fortunate than in this, that so unique a companion should have been ready to devote herself to him with an affection wholly free from egotism or jealousy,—an affection that yearned only to satisfy his subtlest needs, and to transfuse all that was best in herself into his larger being. And indeed that fortunate admixture or influence, whencesoever derived, which raised the race of Wordsworth to poetic fame, was almost more dominant and conspicuous in Dorothy Wordsworth than in the poet himself. "The shooting lights of her wild eyes" reflected to the full the strain of imaginative emotion which was mingled in the poet's nature with that spirit of steadfast and conservative virtue which has already given to the family a Master of Trinity, two Bishops, and other divines and scholars of weight and consideration. In the poet himself the conservative and ecclesiastical tendencies of his character became more and more apparent as advancing years stiffened the movements of the mind. In his sister the ardent element was less restrained ; it showed itself in a most innocent direction, but it brought with it a heavy punishment. Her passion for nature and her affection for her brother led her into mountain rambles which were beyond her strength, and her last years were spent in a condition of physical and mental decay.

But at the time of which we are now speaking there was, perhaps, no one in the world who could have been to the poet such a companion as his sister became. She had not, of course, his grasp of mind or his poetic power ; but her sensitiveness to nature was quite as keen as his, and her disposition resembled his " with sunshine added to daylight."

> Birds in the bower, and lambs in the green field,
> Could they have known her, would have loved ; methought
> Her very presence such a sweetness breathed,

> That flowers, and trees, and even the silent hills,
> And everything she looked on, should have had
> An intimation how she bore herself
> Towards them, and to all creatures.

Her journal of a tour in Scotland, and her description of a week on Ullswater, affixed to Wordsworth's *Guide to the Lakes,*—diaries not written for publication but merely to communicate her own delight to intimate friends at a distance,—are surely indescribably attractive in their naive and tender feeling, combined with a delicacy of insight into natural beauty which was almost a new thing in the history of the world. If we compare, for instance, any of her descriptions of the Lakes with Southey's, we see the difference between mere literary skill, which can now be rivalled in many quarters, and that sympathetic intuition which comes of love alone. Even if we compare her with Gray, whose short notice of Cumberland bears on every page the stamp of a true poet, we are struck by the way in which Miss Wordsworth's tenderness for all living things gives character and pathos to her landscapes, and evokes from the wildest solitude some note that thrills the heart.

> She gave me eyes, she gave me ears,
> And humble cares, and delicate fears;
> A heart the fountain of sweet tears;
> And love, and thought, and joy.

The cottage life in her brother's company which we have seen Miss Wordsworth picturing to herself with girlish ardour, was destined to be realized no long time afterwards, thanks to the unlooked-for outcome of another friendship. If the poet's sister was his first admirer, Raisley Calvert may fairly claim the second place. Calvert was the son of the steward of the Duke of Norfolk, who possessed

large estates in Cumberland. He attached himself to
Wordsworth, and in 1793 and 1794 the friends were
much together. Calvert was then attacked by consump-
tion, and Wordsworth nursed him with patient care. It
was found at his death that he had left his friend
a legacy of 900*l*. "The act," says Wordsworth,
" was done entirely from a confidence on his part that I
had powers and attainments which might be of use to
mankind. Upon the interest of the 900*l*.—400*l*. being
laid out in annuity—with 200*l*. deducted from the principal, and 100*l*. a legacy to my sister, and 100*l*. more which
the *Lyrical Ballads* have brought me, my sister and I
contrived to live seven years, nearly eight."
      Trusting in this small capital, and with nothing to look
to in the future except the uncertain prospect of the pay-
ment of Lord Lonsdale's debt to the family, Wordsworth
settled with his sister at Racedown, near Crewkerne, in
Dorsetshire, in the autumn of 1795, the choice of this
locality being apparently determined by the offer of a
cottage on easy terms. Here, in the first home which he
had possessed, Wordsworth's steady devotion to poetry
began. He had already, in 1792,[1] published two little
poems, the *Evening Walk* and *Descriptive Sketches*, which
Miss Wordsworth (to whom the *Evening Walk* was
addressed) criticises with candour in a letter to the same
friend (Forncett, February 1792) :—
      "The scenes which he describes have been viewed with
a poet's eye, and are portrayed with a poet's pencil ; and
the poems contain many passages exquisitely beautiful;
but they also contain many faults, the chief of which are
obscurity and a too frequent use of some particular expres-

  [1] The *Memoirs* say in 1793, but the following MS. letter of
1792 speaks of them as already published.

sions and uncommon words ; for instance, *moveless*, which
he applies in a sense, if not new, at least different from its
ordinary one. By moveless,' when applied to the swan, he
means that sort of motion which is smooth without agitation ; it is a very beautiful epithet, but ought to have
been cautiously used. The word *viewless* also is introduced far too often. I regret exceedingly that he did not
submit the works to the inspection of some friend before
their publication, and he also joins with me in this
regret."

These poems show a careful and minute observation of
nature, but their versification—still reminding us of the
imitators of Pope—has little originality or charm. They
attracted the admiration of Coleridge, but had no further
success.

At Racedown Wordsworth finished *Guilt and Sorrow*,
a poem gloomy in tone and written mainly in his period
of depression and unrest,—and wrote a tragedy called *The
Borderers*, of which only a few lines show any promise of
future excellence. He then wrote *The Ruined Cottage*,
now incorporated in the First Book of the *Excursion*. This
poem, on a subject thoroughly suited to his powers, was
his first work of merit ; and Coleridge, who visited the
quiet household in June 1797, pronounces this poem
"superior, I hesitate not to aver, to anything in
our language which in any way resembles it." In
July 1797 the Wordsworths removed to Alfoxden, a
large house in Somersetshire, near Netherstowey, where
Coleridge was at that time living. Here Wordsworth
added to his income by taking as pupil a young boy, the
hero of the trifling poem *Anecdote for Fathers*, a son of
Mr. Basil Montagu ; and here he composed many of his
smaller pieces. He has described the origin of the

Ancient Mariner and the *Lyrical Ballads* in a well-known
passage, part of which I must here repeat :—

" In the autumn of 1797, Mr. Coleridge, my sister, and myself started from Alfoxden pretty late in the afternoon, with
a view to visit Linton, and the Valley of Stones near to it; and
as our united funds were very small, we agreed to defray the
expense of the tour by writing a poem, to be sent to the *New
Monthly Magazine.* In the course of this walk was planned
the poem of the *Ancient Mariner*, founded on a dream, as Mr.
Coleridge said, of his friend Mr. Cruikshank. Much the greatest
part of the story was Mr. Coleridge's invention ; but certain
parts I suggested ; for example, some crime was to be committed
which was to bring upon the Old Navigator, as Coleridge afterwards delighted to call him, the spectral persecution, as a consequence of that crime and his own wanderings. I had been
reading in Shelvocke's *Voyages*, a day or two before, that, while
doubling Cape Horn they frequently saw albatrosses in that
latitude, the largest sort of sea-fowl, some extending their wings
twelve or thirteen feet. ' Suppose,' said I, ' you represent him
as having killed one of these birds on entering the South Sea,
and that the tutelary spirits of these regions take upon them
to avenge the crime. The incident was thought fit for the
purpose, and adopted accordingly. I also suggested the naviga-
tion of the ship by the dead man, but do not recollect that I
had anything more to do with the scheme of the poem. We
began the composition together, on that to me memorable evening. I furnished two or three lines at the beginning of the
poem, in particular—

> And listened like a three years' child ;
> The Mariner had his will.

As we endeavoured to proceed conjointly our respective manners proved so widely different, that it would have been quite
presumptuous in me to do anything but separate from an under-
taking upon which I could only have been a clog. The *Ancient
Mariner* grew and grew, till it became too important for our
first object, which was limited to our expectation of five pounds;

and we began to think of a volume, which was to consist, as
Mr. Coleridge has told the world, of poems chiefly on supernatural subjects, taken from common life, but looked at, as
much as might be, through an imaginative medium."

The volume of *Lyrical Ballads*, whose first beginnings
have here been traced, was published in the autumn of
1798, by Mr. Cottle, at Bristol. This volume contained
several poems which have been justly blamed for triviality,
—as *The Thorn, Goody Blake, The Idiot Boy ;* several
in which, as in *Simon Lee*, triviality is mingled with
much real pathos ; and some, as *Expostulation and Reply*
and *The Tables Turned*, which are of the very essence of
Wordsworth's nature. It is hardly too much to say, that
if these two last-named poems—to the careless eye so
slight and trifling—were all that had remained from
Wordsworth's hand, they would have "spoken to the
comprehending" of a new individuality, as distinct and
unmistakeable in its way as that which Sappho has left
engraven on the world for ever in words even fewer than
these. And the volume ended with a poem which Wordsworth composed in 1798, in one day, during a tour with
his sister to Tintern and Chepstow. The *Lines written
above Tintern Abbey* have become, as it were, the *locus
classicus* or consecrated formulary of the Wordsworthian
faith. They say in brief what it is the work of the poet's
biographer to say in detail.

As soon as this volume was published Wordsworth and
his sister sailed for Hamburg, in the hope that their
imperfect acquaintance with the German language might
be improved by the heroic remedy of a winter at Goslar.
But at Goslar they do not seem to have made any acquaintances, and their self-improvement consisted mainly in
reading German books to themselves. The four months

D

spent at Goslar, however, were the very bloom of Wordsworth's poetic career. Through none of his poems has
the peculiar loveliness of English scenery and English girlhood shone more delicately than through those which
came to him as he paced the frozen gardens of that desolate city. Here it was that he wrote *Lucy Gray*, and
Ruth, and *Nutting*, and the *Poet's Epitaph*, and other
poems known now to most men as possessing in its full
fragrance his especial charm. And here it was that the
memory of some emotion prompted the lines on *Lucy*. Of
the history of that emotion he has told us nothing; I
forbear, therefore, to inquire concerning it, or even to
speculate. That it was to the poet's honour I do not
doubt; but who ever learned such secrets rightly? or who
should wish to learn? It is best to leave the sanctuary of
all hearts inviolate, and to respect the reserve not only of
the living but of the dead. Of these poems, almost
alone, Wordsworth in his autobiographical notes has said
nothing whatever. One of them he suppressed for years,
and printed only in a later volume. One can, indeed, well
imagine that there may be poems which a man may be
willing to give to the world only in the hope that their
pathos will be, as it were, protected by its own intensity,
and that those who are worthiest to comprehend will be
least disposed to discuss them.

The autobiographical notes on his own works above
alluded to were dictated by the poet to his friend Miss
Isabella Fenwick, at her urgent request, in 1843, and pre-
serve many interesting particulars as to the circumstances
under which each poem was composed. They are to be
found printed entire among Wordsworth's prose works,
and I shall therefore cite them only occasionally. Of
Lucy Gray, for instance, he says,—

"It was founded on a circumstance told me by my sister, of a little girl who, not far from Halifax, in Yorkshire, was bewildered in a snowstorm. Her footsteps were tracked by her parents to the middle of the lock of a canal, and no other vestige of her, backward or forward, could be traced. The body, however, was found in the canal. The way in which the incident was treated, and the spiritualizing of the character, might furnish hints for contrasting the imaginative influences which I have endeavoured to throw over common life, with Crabbe's matter-of-fact style of handling subjects of the same kind."

And of the *Lines written in Germany,* 1798-9,—

"A bitter winter it was when these verses were composed by the side of my sister, in our lodgings, at a draper's house, in the romantic imperial town of Goslar, on the edge of the Hartz forest. So severe was the cold of this winter, that when we passed out of the parlour warmed by the stove our cheeks were struck by the air as by cold iron. I slept in a room over a passage that was not ceiled. The people of the house used to say, rather unfeelingly, that they expected I should be frozen to death some night; but with the protection of a pelisse lined with fur, and a dog's-skin bonnet, such as was worn by the peasants, I walked daily on the ramparts or on a sort of public ground or garden, in which was a pond. Here I had no companion but a kingfisher, a beautiful creature that used to glance by me. I consequently became much attached to it. During these walks I composed *The Poet's Epitaph.*"

Seldom has there been a more impressive instance of the contrast, familiar to biographers, between the apparent insignificance and the real importance of their hero in undistinguished youth. To any one considering Wordsworth as he then was,—a rough and somewhat stubborn young man, who, in nearly thirty years of life, had seemed alternately to idle without grace and to study without advantage,— it might well have seemed incredible that he could have anything new or valuable to communicate to mankind.

D 2

Where had been his experience? or where was the indication of that wealth of sensuous emotion which in such a nature as Keats' seems almost to dispense with experience and to give novelty by giving vividness to such passions as are known to all? If Wordsworth were to impress mankind it must be, one might have thought, by travelling out of himself altogether—by revealing some such energy of imagination as can create a world of romance and adventure in the shyest heart. But this was not so to be. Already Wordsworth's minor poems had dealt almost entirely with his own feelings, and with the objects actually before his eyes; and it was at Goslar that he planned, and on the day of his quitting Goslar that he began, a much longer poem, whose subject was to be still more intimately personal, being the development of his own mind. This poem, dedicated to Coleridge, and written in the form of a confidence bestowed on an intimate friend, was finished in 1805, but was not published till after the poet's death. Mrs. Wordsworth then named it *The Prelude*, indicating thus the relation which it bears to the *Excursion*—or rather, to the projected poem of the *Recluse*, of which the *Excursion* was to form only the Second out of three Divisions. One Book of the First Division of the *Recluse* was written, but is yet unpublished; the Third Division was never even begun, and "the materials," we are told, "of which it would have been formed have been incorporated, for the most part, in the author's other publications." Nor need this change of plan be regretted : didactic poems admit easily of mutilation ; and all that can be called plot in this series of works is contained in the *Prelude*, in which we see Wordsworth arriving at those convictions which in the *Excursion* he pauses to expound.

It would be too much to say that Wordsworth has

been wholly successful in the attempt—for such the
Prelude virtually is—to write an epic poem on his own
education.   Such a poem must almost necessarily appear
tedious and egoistic, and Wordsworth's manner has not
tact enough to prevent these defects from being felt to the
full.   On the contrary, in his constant desire frugally to
extract, as it were, its full teaching from the minutest
event which has befallen him, he supplements the self-
complacency of the autobiographer with the conscientious
exactness of the moralist, and is apt to insist on trifles
such as lodge in the corners of every man's memory, as if
they were unique lessons vouchsafed to himself alone.

Yet it follows from this very temper of mind that there is
scarcely any autobiography which we can read with such
implicit confidence as the *Prelude*.   In the case of this, as of
so many of Wordsworth's productions, our first dissatisfac-
tion at the form which the poem assumes yields to a recognition of its fitness to express precisely what the poet intends.
Nor are there many men who, in recounting the story of
their own lives, could combine a candour so absolute with
so much of dignity—who could treat their personal history
so impartially as a means of conveying lessons of general
truth—or who, while chronicling such small things, could
remain so great.   The *Prelude* is a book of good augury
for human nature.   We feel in reading it as if the stock of
mankind were sound.   The soul seems going on from
strength to strength by the mere development of her
inborn power.   And the scene with which the poem at
once opens and concludes—the return to the Lake country
as to a permanent and satisfying home—places the poet at
last amid his true surroundings, and leaves us to contem-
plate him as completed by a harmony without him, which
he of all men most needed to evoke the harmony within.

CHAPTER IV.

THE ENGLISH LAKES.

THE lakes and mountains of Cumberland, Westmoreland, and Lancashire, are singularly fitted to supply such elements of moral sustenance as Nature's aspects can afford to man. There are, indeed, many mountain regions of greater awfulness; but prospects of ice and terror should be a rare stimulant rather than an habitual food; and the physical difficulties inseparable from immense elevations depress the inhabitant and preoccupy the traveller. There are many lakes under a more lustrous sky; but the healthy activities of life demand a scene brilliant without languor, and a beauty which can refresh and satisfy rather than lull or overpower. Without advancing any untenable claim to British pre-eminence in the matter of scenery, we may, perhaps, follow on both these points the judgment which Wordsworth has expressed in his *Guide to the Lakes*, a work which condenses the results of many years of intimate observation.

"Our tracts of wood and water," he says, "are almost diminutive in comparison (with Switzerland); therefore, as far as sublimity is dependent upon absolute bulk and height, and atmospherical influences in connexion with these, it is obvious that there can be no rivalship. But a short residence among the British mountains will furnish

abundant proof, that, after a certain point of elevation,
viz., that which allows of compact and fleecy clouds
settling upon, or sweeping over, the summits, the sense of
sublimity depends more upon form and relation of objects
to each other than upon their actual magnitude ; and that
an elevation of 3000 feet is sufficient to call forth in a
most impressive degree the creative, and magnifying, and
softening powers of the atmosphere."

And again, as to climate ; " The rain," he says, " here
comes down heartily, and is frequently succeeded by clear
bright weather, when every brook is vocal, and every
torrent sonorous ; brooks and torrents which are never
muddy even in the heaviest floods. Days of unsettled
weather, with partial showers, are very frequent ; but
the showers, darkening or brightening as they fly
from hill to hill, are not less grateful to the eye than
finely interwoven passages of gay and sad music are
touching to the ear. Vapours exhaling from the lakes
and meadows after sunrise in a hot season, or in moist
weather brooding upon the heights, or descending towards
the valleys with inaudible motion, give a visionary character to everything around them ; and are in themselves
so beautiful as to dispose us to enter into the feelings of
those simple nations (such as the Laplanders of this day)
by whom they are taken for guardian deities of the
mountains ; or to sympathize with others who have fancied these delicate apparitions to be the spirits of their
departed ancestors. Akin to these are fleecy clouds rest-
ing upon the hill-tops ; they are not easily managed in
picture, with their accompaniments of blue sky, but how
glorious are they in nature ! how pregnant with imagination for the poet ! And the height of the Cumbrian mountains is sufficient to exhibit daily and hourly instances of

those mysterious attachments. Such clouds, cleaving to
their stations, or lifting up suddenly their glittering heads
from behind rocky barriers, or hurrying out of sight with
speed of the sharpest edge, will often tempt an inhabitant
to congratulate himself on belonging to a country of mists
and clouds and storms, and make him think of the blank
sky of Egypt, and of the cerulean vacancy of Italy, as an
unanimated and even a sad spectacle."

The consciousness of a preceding turmoil brings home
to us best the sense of perfect peace ; and a climate accustomed to storm-cloud and tempest can melt sometimes
into "a day as still as heaven" with a benignant tranquillity which calmer regions can scarcely know. Such a day
Wordsworth has described in language of such delicate
truth and beauty as only a long and intimate love can
inspire :

"It has been said that in human life there are moments
worth ages. In a more subdued tone of sympathy may we
affirm, that in the climate of England there are, for the lover of
Nature, days which are worth whole months, I might say, even
years. One of these favoured days sometimes occurs in spring-
time, when that soft air is breathing over the blossoms and new-
born verdure which inspired Buchanan with his beautiful Ode
to the First of May ; the air which, in the luxuriance of his fancy,
he likens to that of the golden age,—to that which gives motion
to the funereal cypresses on the banks of Lethe ; to the air
which is to salute beatified spirits when expiatory fires shall
have consumed the earth with all her habitations. But it is
in autumn that days of such affecting influence most frequently
intervene. The atmosphere seems refined, and the sky rendered
more crystalline, as the vivifying heat of the year abates ; the
lights and shadows are more delicate ; the colouring is richer
and more finely harmonized ; and, in this season of stillness,
the ear being unoccupied, or only gently excited, the sense of
vision becomes more susceptible of its appropriate enjoyments.

A resident in a country like this which we are treating of will agree with me that the presence of a lake is indispensable to exhibit in perfection the beauty of one of these days; and he must have experienced, while looking on the unruffled waters, that the imagination by their aid is carried into recesses of feeling otherwise impenetrable. The reason of this is, that the heavens are not only brought down into the bosom of the earth, but that the earth is mainly looked at, and thought of, through the medium of a purer element. The happiest time is when the equinoctial gales are departed; but their fury may probably be called to mind by the sight of a few shattered boughs, whose leaves do not differ in colour from the faded foliage of the stately oaks from which these relics of the storm depend: all else speaks of tranquillity; not a breath of air, no restlessness of insects, and not a moving object perceptible—except the clouds gliding in the depths of the lake, or the traveller passing along, an inverted image, whose motion seems governed by the quiet of a time to which its archetype, the living person, is perhaps insensible; or it may happen that the figure of one of the larger birds, a raven or a heron, is crossing silently among the reflected clouds, while the voice of the real bird, from the element aloft, gently awakens in the spectator the recollection of appetites and instincts, pursuits and occupations, that deform and agitate the world, yet have no power to prevent nature from putting on an aspect capable of satisfying the most intense cravings for the tranquil, the lovely, and the perfect, to which man, the noblest of her creatures, is subject."

The scene described here is one as exquisite in detail as majestic in general effect. And it is characteristic of the region to which Wordsworth's love was given that there is no corner of it without a meaning and a charm; that the open record of its immemorial past tells us at every turn that all agencies have conspired for loveliness and ruin itself has been benign. A passage of Wordsworth's describing the character of the lake-shores illustrates this fact with loving minuteness.

"Sublimity is the result of nature's first great dealings with the superficies of the Earth ; but the general tendency of her subsequent operations is towards the production of beauty, by a multiplicity of symmetrical parts uniting in a consistent whole. This is everywhere exemplified along the margins of these lakes. Masses of rock, that have been precipitated from the heights into the area of waters, lie in some places like stranded ships, or have acquired the compact structure of jutting piers, or project in little peninsulas crested with native wood. The smallest rivulet, one whose silent influx is scarcely noticeable in a season of dry weather, so faint is the dimple made by it on the surface of the smooth lake, will be found to have been not useless in shaping, by its deposits of gravel and soil in time of flood, a curve that would not otherwise have existed. But the more powerful brooks, encroaching upon the level of the lake, have, in course of time, given birth to ample promontories of sweeping outline, that contrast boldly with the longitudinal base of the steeps on the opposite shore ; while their flat or gently-sloping surfaces never fail to introduce, into the midst of desolation and barrenness, the elements of fertility, even where the habitations of men may not have been raised."

With this we may contrast, as a companion picture, the poet's description of the tarns, or lonely bodies of water, which lie here and there among the hills :

"They are difficult of access and naked ; yet some of them are, in their permanent forms, very grand, and there are accidents of things which would make the meanest of them interesting. At all events, one of these pools is an acceptable sight to the mountain wanderer, not merely as an incident that diversifies the prospect, but as forming in his mind a centre or conspicuous point to which objects, otherwise disconnected or insubordinated, may be referred. Some few have a varied outline, with bold heath-clad promontories ; and as they mostly lie at the foot of a steep precipice, the water, where the sun is not shining upon it, appears black and sullen, and round the margin huge stones and masses of rock are scattered, some defying conjecture as to the means by which they came thither, and others obviously fallen from on high, the contribution of ages ! A not unpleasing sadness is induced by this perplexity, and these images of decay; while the prospect of a body of pure water, unattended with groves and other cheerful rural images by which fresh water is usually accompanied, and unable to give furtherance to the meagre vegetation around it, excites a sense of some repulsive power strongly put forth, and thus deepens the melancholy natural to such scenes."

To those who love to deduce the character of a population from the character of their race and surroundings the peasantry of Cumberland and Westmoreland form an attractive theme. Drawn in great part from the strong Scandinavian stock, they dwell in a land solemn and beautiful as Norway itself, but without Norway's rigour and penury, and with still lakes and happy rivers instead of Norway's inarming melancholy sea. They are a mountain folk; but their mountains are no precipices of insuperable snow, such as keep the dwellers in some Swiss hamlet shut in ignorance and stagnating into idiocy. These barriers divide only to concentrate, and environ only to endear; their guardianship is but enough to give an added unity to each group of kindred homes. And thus it is that the Cumbrian dalesmen have afforded perhaps as near a realization as human fates have yet allowed of the rural society which statesmen desire for their country's greatness. They have given an example of substantial comfort strenuously won; of home affections intensified by independent strength; of isolation without ignorance, and of a shrewd simplicity; of an hereditary virtue which needs no support from fanaticism, and to which honour is more than law.

The school of political economists, moreover, who urge the advantage of a peasant proprietary—of small inde-

pendent holdings,—as at once drawing from the land the
fullest produce and rearing upon it the most vigorous
and provident population,—this school, as is well known,
finds in the *statesmen* of Cumberland one of its favourite
examples. In the days of border-wars, when the first
object was to secure the existence of as many armed men
as possible, in readiness to repel the Scot, the abbeys and
great proprietors in the north readily granted small estates
on military tenure, which tenure, when personal service
in the field was no longer needed, became in most cases
an absolute ownership. The attachment of these *statesmen* to their hereditary estates, the heroic efforts which
they would make to avoid parting with them, formed an
impressive phenomenon in the little world—a world at
once of equality and of conservatism—which was the
scene of Wordsworth's childish years, and which remained
his manhood's ideal.

The growth of large fortunes in England, and the
increased competition for land, has swallowed up many of
these small independent holdings in the extensive pro-
perties of wealthy men. And at the same time the spread
of education, and the improved poor-laws and other
legislation, by raising the condition of other parts of
England, have tended to obliterate the contrast which
was so marked in Wordsworth's day. How marked that
contrast was, a comparison of Crabbe's poems with
Wordsworth's will sufficiently indicate. Both are true
painters ; but while in the one we see poverty as something gross and degrading, and the *Tales of the Village*
stand out from a background of pauperism and crime ; in
the other picture poverty means nothing worse than
privation, and the poet in the presence of the most tragic
outcast of fortune could still

> Have laughed himself to scorn, to find
> In that decrepit man so firm a mind.

Nay, even when a state far below the *Leech-Gatherer's* has
been reached, and mind and body alike are in their last decay, the life of the *Old Cumberland Beggar*, at one remove
from nothingness, has yet a dignity and a usefulness of its
own. His fading days are passed in no sad asylum of
vicious or gloomy age, but amid neighbourly kindnesses,
and in the sanity of the open air ; and a life that is reduced to its barest elements has yet a hold on the liberality
of nature and the affections of human hearts.

So long as the inhabitants of a region so solitary and
beautiful have neither many arts nor many wishes, save
such as the Nature which they know has suggested, and
their own handiwork can satisfy, so long are their presence
and habitations likely to be in harmony with the scenes
around them. Nay, man's presence is almost always
needed to draw out the full meaning of Nature, to illustrate
her bounty by his glad well-being and to hint by his con-
trivances of precaution at her might and terror. Wordsworth's description of the cottages of Cumberland depicts
this unconscious adaptation of man's abode to his surroundings, with an eye which may be called at pleasure that of
painter or of poet.

" The dwelling-houses, and contiguous outhouses, are in many
instances of the colour of the native rock out of which they have
been built ; but frequently the dwelling—or Fire-house, as it is
ordinarily called—has been distinguished from the barn or byre
by roughcast and whitewash, which, as the inhabitants are not
hasty in renewing it, in a few years acquires by the influence of
weather a tint at once sober and variegated. As these houses
have been, from father to son, inhabited by persons engaged in
the same occupations, yet necessarily with changes in their

circumstances, they have received without incongruity additions and accommodations adapted to the needs of each successive occupant, who, being for the most part proprietor, was at liberty to follow his own fancy, so that these humble dwellings remind the contemplative spectator of a production of Nature, and may (using a strong expression) rather be said to have grown than to have been erected—to have risen, by an instinct of their own, out of the native rock—so little is there in them of formality, such is their wildness and beauty.

" These dwellings, mostly built, as has been said, of rough unhewn stone, are roofed with slates, which were rudely taken from the quarry before the present art of splitting them was understood, and are therefore rough and uneven in their surface, so that both the coverings and sides of the houses have furnished places of rest for the seeds of lichens, mosses, ferns and flowers. Hence buildings, which in their very form call to mind the processes of Nature, do thus, clothed in part with a vegetable garb, appear to be received into the bosom of the living principle of things, as it acts and exists among the woods and fields, and by their colour and their shape affectingly direct the thoughts to that tranquil course of nature and simplicity along which the humble-minded inhabitants have through so many generations been led. Add the little garden with its shed for bee-hives, its small bed of potherbs, and its borders and patches of flowers for Sunday posies, with sometimes a choice few too much prized to be plucked; an orchard of proportioned size; a cheesepress, often supported by some tree near the door; a cluster of embowering sycamores for summer shade, with a tall fir through which the winds sing when other trees are leafless ; the little rill or household spout murmuring in all seasons,—combine these incidents and images together, and you have the representative idea of a mountain cottage in this country—so beautifully formed in itself, and so richly adorned by the hand of Nature."

These brief descriptions may suffice to indicate the general character of a district which in Wordsworth's early days had a distinctive unity which he was the first fully to appreciate, which was at its best during his long

lifetime, and which has already begun to disappear. The
mountains had waited long for a full adoration, an intelligent worship. At last " they were enough beloved."
And if now the changes wrought around them recall too
often the poet's warning, how

> All that now delights thee, from the day
> On which it should be touched, shall melt, and melt away,—

yet they have gained something which cannot be taken
from them. Not mines, nor railways, nor monster ex-
cursions, nor reservoirs, nor Manchester herself, " toute
entière à sa proie attachée," can deprive lake and hill of
Wordsworth's memory, and the love which once they
knew.

Wordsworth's life was from the very first so ordered as
to give him the most complete and intimate knowledge
both of district and people. There was scarcely a mile of
ground in the Lake country over which he had not
wandered ; scarcely a prospect which was not linked with
his life by some tie of memory. Born at Cockermouth,
on the outskirts of the district, his mind was gradually
led on to its beauty ; and his first recollections were of
Derwent's grassy holms and rocky falls, with Skiddaw,
"bronzed with deepest radiance," towering in the eastern
sky. Sent to school at Hawkshead at eight years old,
Wordsworth's scene was transferred to the other extremity of the lake district. It was in this quaint old
town, on the banks of Esthwaite Water, that the " fair
seed-time of his soul" was passed ; it was here that his
boyish delight in exercise and adventure grew, and melted
in its turn into a more impersonal yearning, a deeper
absorption into the beauty and the wonder of the world.
And even the records of his boyish amusements come

to us each on a background of Nature's majesty and calm. Setting springs for woodcock on the grassy moors at night, at nine years old, he feels himself "a trouble to the peace" that dwells among the moon and stars overhead; and when he has appropriated a woodcock caught by somebody else, "sounds of undistinguishable motion" embody the viewless pursuit of Nemesis among the solitary hills. In the perilous search for the raven's nest, as he hangs on the face of the naked crags of Yewdale, he feels for the first time that sense of detachment from external things which a position of strange unreality will often force on the mind.

> Oh, at that time
> When on the perilous ridge I hung alone,
> With what strange utterance did the loud dry wind
> Blow through my ear! the sky seemed not a sky
> Of earth—and with what motion moved the clouds!

The innocent rapine of *nutting* taught him to feel that there is a spirit in the woods—a presence which too rude a touch of ours will desecrate and destroy.

The neighbouring lakes of Coniston, Esthwaite, Windermere, have left similar traces of the gradual upbuilding of his spirit. It was on a promontory on Coniston that the sun's last rays, gilding the eastern hills above which he had first appeared, suggested the boy's first impulse of spontaneous poetry, in the resolve that, wherever life should lead him, his last thoughts should fall on the scenes where his childhood was passing now. It was on Esthwaite that the " huge peak " of Wetherlam, following him (as it seemed) as he rowed across the starlit water, suggested the dim conception of " unknown modes of being," and a life that is not ours. It was round Esthwaite that the boy used to wander with a friend at early dawn, rejoicing in the

charm of words in tuneful order, and repeating together
their favourite verses, till "sounds of exultation echoed
through the groves." It was on Esthwaite that the band
of skaters "hissed along the polished ice in games con-
federate," from which Wordsworth would sometimes
withdraw himself and pause suddenly in full career, to
feel in that dizzy silence the mystery of a rolling world.

A passage, less frequently quoted, in describing a boating
excursion on Windermere illustrates the effect of some
small point of human interest in concentrating and
realising the diffused emotion which radiates from a scene
of beauty :

> But, ere nightfall,
> When in our pinnace we returned at leisure
> Over the shadowy lake, and to the beach
> Of some small island steered our course with one,
> The minstrel of the troop, and left him there,
> And rowed off gently, while he blew his flute
> Alone upon the rock—oh, then the calm
> And dead still water lay upon my mind
> Even with a weight of pleasure, and the sky,
> Never before so beautiful, sank down
> Into my heart, and held me like a dream !

The passage which describes the schoolboy's call to the
owls—the lines of which Coleridge said that he should
have exclaimed "Wordsworth ! " if he had met them
running wild in the deserts of Arabia,—paint a somewhat
similar rush of feeling with a still deeper charm. The
"gentle shock of mild surprise " which in the pauses of the
birds' jocund din *carries far into his heart the sound of
mountain torrents*—the very mingling of the grotesque and
the majestic—brings home the contrast between our transitory energies and the mystery around us which returns
ever the same to the moments when we pause and are at
peace.

E

It is round the two small lakes of Grasmere and
Rydal that the memories of Wordsworth are most thickly
clustered. On one or other of these lakes he lived for
fifty years,—the first half of the present century ; and
there is not in all that region a hillside walk or winding
valley which has not heard him murmuring out his verses
as they slowly rose from his heart. The cottage at Townend, Grasmere, where he first settled, is now surrounded
by the out-buildings of a busy hotel, and the noisy stream
of traffic, and the sight of the many villas which spot the
valley, give a new pathos to the sonnet in which Wordsworth deplores the alteration which even his own residence might make in the simplicity of the lonely scene.

> Well may'st thou halt, and gaze with brightening eye !
> The lovely Cottage in the guardian nook
> Hath stirred thee deeply ; with its own dear brook,
> Its own small pasture, almost its own sky !
> But covet not the Abode : forbear to sigh,
> As many do, repining while they look ;
> Intruders—who would tear from Nature's book
> This precious leaf with harsh impiety.
> Think what the home must be if it were thine,
> Even thine, though few thy wants ! Roof, window, door,
> The very flowers are sacred to the Poor,
> The roses to the porch which they entwine :
> Yea, all that now enchants thee, from the day
> On which it should be touched, would melt, and melt away.

The *Poems on the Naming of Places* belong for the
most part to this neighbourhood. *Emma's Dell* on Easdale
Beck, *Point Rash-Judgment* on the eastern shore of Grasmere, *Mary's Pool* in Rydal Park, *William's Peak* on Stone
Arthur, *Joanna's Rock* on the banks of Rotha, and *John's
Grove* near White Moss Common, have been identified by
the loving search of those to whom every memorial of
that simple-hearted family group has still a charm.

It is on Greenhead Ghyll—"upon the forest-side in Grasmere Vale"—that the poet has laid the scene of *Michael*, the poem which paints with such detailed fidelity both the inner and the outward life of a typical Westmoreland "statesman." And the upper road from Grasmere to Rydal, superseded now by the road along the lake side, and left as a winding footpath among rock and fern, was one of his most habitual haunts. Of another such haunt his friend Lady Richardson says, "The *Prelude* was chiefly composed in a green mountain terrace, on the Easdale side of Helm Crag, known by the name of Under Lancrigg, a place which he used to say he knew by heart. The ladies sat at their work on the hill-side, while he walked to and fro on the smooth green mountain turf, humming out his verses to himself, and then repeating them to his sympathising and ready scribes, to be noted down on the spot, and transcribed at home."

The neighbourhood of the poet's later home at Rydal Mount is equally full of associations. Two of the *Evening Voluntaries* were composed by the side of Rydal Mere. The *Wild Duck's Nest* was on one of the Rydal islands. It was on the fells of Loughrigg that the poet's fancy loved to plant an imperial castle. And *Wansfell's* green slope still answers with many a change of glow and shadow to the radiance of the sinking sun.

Hawkshead and Rydal, then, may be considered as the poet's principal centres, and the scenery in their neighbourhood has received his most frequent attention. The Duddon, a seldom-visited stream on the south-west border of the Lake-district, has been traced by him from source to outfall in a series of sonnets. Langdale, and Little Langdale with Blea Tarn lying in it, form the principal scene of the discourses in the *Excursion*. The more distant lakes and mountains were often visited and are often alluded to. The scene of *The Brothers*, for example, is laid in Ennerdale; and the index of the minor poems will supply other instances. But it is chiefly round two lines of road leading from Grasmere that Wordsworth's associations cluster,—the route over Dunmailraise, which led him to Keswick, to Coleridge and Southey at Greta Hall, and to other friends in that neighbourhood; and the route over Kirkstone, which led him to Ullswater, and the friendly houses of Patterdale, Hallsteads, and Lowther Castle. The first of these two routes was that over which the *Waggoner* plied; it skirts the lovely shore of Thirlmere,—a lonely sheet of water, of exquisite irregularity of outline, and fringed with delicate verdure, which the Corporation of Manchester has lately bought to embank it into a reservoir. *Dedecorum pretiosus emptor!* This lake was a favourite haunt of Wordsworth's; and upon a rock on its margin, where he and Coleridge, coming from Keswick and Grasmere, would often meet, the two poets, with the other members of Wordsworth's loving household group, inscribed the initial letters of their names. To the "monumental power" of this Rock of Names Wordsworth appeals, in lines written when the happy company who engraved them had already been severed by distance and death:

> O thought of pain,
> That would impair it or profane!
> And fail not Thou, loved Rock, to keep
> Thy charge when we are laid asleep.

The rock may still be seen, but is to be submerged in the new reservoir. In the vale of Keswick itself, Applethwaite, Skiddaw, St. Herbert's Island, Lodore,

are commemorated in sonnets or inscriptions. And the
Borrowdale yew-trees have inspired some of the poet's
noblest lines,—lines breathing all the strange forlornness
of Glaramara's solitude, and the withering vault of shade.
The route from Rydal to Ullswater is still more thickly
studded with poetic allusions. The *Pass of Kirkstone*
is the theme of a characteristic ode; Grisdale Tarn and
Helvellyn recur again and again; and Aira Force was
one of the spots which the poet best loved to describe, as
well as to visit. It was on the shores of Further Gowbarrow that the *Daffodils* danced beneath the trees.
These references might be much further multiplied,
and the loving diligence of disciples has set before
us "the Lake-district as interpreted by Wordsworth"
through a multitude of details. But enough has been
said to show how completely the poet had absorbed the
influences of his dwelling-place; how unique a representative he had become of the lovely district of his birth;
how he had made it subject to him by comprehending it,
and his own by love.

He visited other countries and described other scenes.
Scotland, Wales, Switzerland, France, Germany, Italy,
have all a place in his works. His familiarity with other
scenery helped him, doubtless, to a better appreciation of
the lake country than he could have gained had he never
left it. And, on the other hand, like Cæsar in Gaul, or
Wellington in the Peninsula, it was because he had so
complete a grasp of this chosen base of operations that he
was able to come, to see, and to make his own, so swiftly
and unfailingly elsewhere. Happy are those whose deep-
rooted memories cling like his about some stable home!
whose notion of the world around them has expanded from
some prospect of happy tranquillity, instead of being drawn

at random from the confusing city's roar ! Happier still if
that early picture be of one of those rare scenes which
have inspired poets and prophets with the retrospective
day-dream of a patriarchal, or a golden, age; of some plot
of ground like the Ithaca of Odysseus, τρηχεῖ, ἀλλ᾽ ἀγαθὴ
κουροτρόφος, " rough, but a nurse of *men ;*" of some life
like that which a poet of kindred spirit to Wordsworth's
saw half in vision, half in reality, among the husbandmen
of the Italian hills :—

> Peace, peace is theirs, and life no fraud that knows,
> Wealth as they will, and when they will, repose :
> On many a hill the happy homesteads stand,
> The living lakes through many a vale expand;
> Cool glens are there, and shadowy caves divine,
> Deep sleep, and far-off voices of the kine ;—
> From moor to moor the exulting wild deer stray ;—
> The strenuous youth are strong and sound as they ;
> One reverence still the untainted race inspires,
> God their first thought, and after God their sires ;—
> These last discerned Astræa's flying hem,
> And Virtue's latest footsteps walked with them.

CHAPTER V.

WITH Wordsworth's settlement at Townend, Grasmere, in the closing days of the last century, the external events of his life may be said to come to an end. Even his marriage to Miss Mary Hutchinson, of Penrith, on October 4, 1802, was not so much an importation into his existence of new emotion, as a development and intensification of feelings which had long been there. This marriage was the crowning stroke of Wordsworth's felicity—the poetic recompense for his steady advocacy of all simple and noble things. When he wished to illustrate the true dignity and delicacy of rustic lives he was always accustomed to refer to the Cumbrian folk. And now it seemed that Cumberland requited him for his praises with her choicest boon; found for him in the country town of Penrith, and from the small and obscure circle of his connexions and acquaintance,—nay, from the same dame's school in which he was taught to read,—a wife such as neither rank nor young beauty nor glowing genius enabled his brother bards to win.

Mrs. Wordsworth's poetic appreciativeness, manifest to all who knew her, is attested by the poet's assertion that two of the best lines in the poem of *The Daffodils—*

They flash upon that inward eye
Which is the bliss of solitude,—

were of her composition.   And in all other matters, from
the highest to the lowest, she was to him a true helpmate,
a companion "dearer far than life and light are dear,"
and able "in his steep march to uphold him to the end."
Devoted to her husband, she nevertheless welcomed not
only without jealousy but with delight the household
companionship through life of the sister who formed
so large an element in his being.   Admiring the poet's
genius to the full, and following the workings of his mind
with a sympathy that never tired, she nevertheless was
able to discern, and with unobtrusive care to hide or avert,
those errors of manner into which retirement and self-
absorption will betray even the gentlest spirit.   It speaks,
perhaps, equally well for Wordsworth's character that this
tendency to a lengthy insistance, in general conversation,
on his own feelings and ideas is the worst charge that can
be brought against him ; and for Mrs. Wordsworth's, that
her simple and rustic upbringing had gifted her with a
manner so gracious and a tact so ready that in her
presence all things could not but go well.

The life which the young couple led was one of primitive simplicity.   In some respects it was even less
luxurious than that of the peasants around them.   They
drank water, and ate the simplest fare.   Miss Wordsworth
had long rendered existence possible for her brother on
the narrowest of means by her unselfish energy and skill
in household management ; and "plain living and high
thinking" were equally congenial to the new inmate of
the frugal home.   Wordsworth gardened ; and all together,
or oftenest the poet and his sister, wandered almost daily
over the neighbouring hills.   Narrow means did not pre-

vent them from offering a generous welcome to their few
friends, especially Coleridge and his family, who repeatedly
stayed for months under Wordsworth's roof. Miss Wordsworth's unpublished letters breathe the very spirit of hospi-
tality in their naive details of the little sacrifices gladly
made for the sake of the presence of these honoured
guests. But for the most part their life was solitary and
uneventful. Books they had few ; neighbours almost
none ; and Miss Wordsworth's diary of these early years
describes a life seldom paralleled in its intimate dependence on external nature. I take, almost at random, her
account of a single day. "November 24, 1801. Read
Chaucer. We walked by Gell's cottage. As we were
going along we were stopped at once, at the distance, perhaps, of fifty yards from our favourite birch-tree ; it was
yielding to the gust of wind, with all its tender twigs ;
the sun shone upon it, and it glanced in the wind like a
flying sunshiny shower. It was a tree in shape, with
stem and branches ; but it was like a spirit of water.
After our return William read Spenser to us, and then
walked to John's Grove. Went to meet W." And from
an unpublished letter of Miss Wordsworth's, of about the
same period (September 10, 1800), I extract her description of the new home. "We are daily more delighted
with Grasmere and its neighbourhood. Our walks are
perpetually varied, and we are more fond of the mountains
as our acquaintance with them increases. We have a boat
upon the lake, and a small orchard and smaller garden,
which, as it is the work of our own hands, we regard with
pride and partiality. Our cottage is quite large enough
for us, though very small ; and we have made it neat and
comfortable within doors ; and it looks very nice on the
outside ; for though the roses and honeysuckles which we

have planted against it are only of this year's growth, yet
it is covered all over with green leaves and scarlet flowers ;
for we have trained scarlet beans upon threads, which are
not only exceedingly beautiful but very useful, as their
produce is immense. We have made a lodging-room of
the parlour below stairs, which has a stone floor, therefore
we have covered it all over with matting. We sit in a
room above stairs, and we have one lodging-room with
two single beds, a sort of lumber-room, and a small low
unceiled room, which I have papered with newspapers,
and in which we have put a small bed. Our servant is
an old woman of sixty years of age, whom we took partly
out of charity. She was very ignorant, very foolish, and
very difficult to teach. But the goodness of her disposition, and the great convenience we should find if my
perseverance was successful, induced me to go on."

The sonnets entitled *Personal Talk* give a vivid picture
of the blessings of such seclusion. There are many minds
which will echo the exclamation with which the poet
dismisses his visitors and their gossip :

> Better than such discourse doth silence long,
> Long barren silence, square with my desire ;
> To sit without emotion, hope, or aim,
> In the loved presence of my cottage fire,
> And listen to the flapping of the flame,
> Or kettle whispering its faint undersong.

Many will look with envy on a life which has thus
decisively cut itself loose from the world ; which is secure
from the influx of those preoccupations, at once distracting
and nugatory, which deaden the mind to all other stimulus,
and split the river of life into channels so minute that it
loses itself in the sand.

> Hence have I genial seasons ; hence have I
> Smooth passions, smooth discourse, and joyous thought.

Left to herself, the mind can expatiate in those kingdoms
of the spirit bequeathed to us by past generations and
distant men, which to the idle are but a garden of idleness,
but to those who choose it become a true possession and
an ever widening home. Among those "nobler loves and
nobler cares" there is excitement without reaction, there
is an unwearied and impersonal joy—a joy which can
only be held cheap because it is so abundant, and can
only disappoint us through our own incapacity to contain
it. These delights of study and of solitude Wordsworth
enjoyed to the full. In no other poet, perhaps, have the
poet's heightened sensibilities been productive of a pleasure so unmixed with pain. The wind of his emotions
blew right abaft ; he "swam smoothly in the stream of
his nature, and lived but one man."

The blessing of meditative and lonely hours must of
course be purchased by corresponding limitations. Wordsworth's conception of human character retained to the end
an extreme simplicity. Many of life's most impressive
phenomena were hid from his eyes. He never encountered any of those rare figures whose aspect seems to
justify all traditions of pomp and pre-eminence when
they appear amid stately scenes as with a natural sove-
reignty. He neither achieved nor underwent any of those
experiences which can make all high romance seem a part
of memory, and bestow as it were a password and introduction into the very innermost of human fates. On
the other hand, he almost wholly escaped those suffer-
ings which exceptional natures must needs derive from
too close a contact with this commonplace world. It was
not his lot—as it has been the lot of so many poets—
to move amongst mankind at once as an intimate and a
stranger; to travel from disillusionment to disillusionment

and from regret to regret; to construct around him a world of ideal beings, who crumble into dust at his touch; to hope from them what they can neither understand nor accomplish, to lavish on them what they can never repay. Such pain, indeed, may become a discipline; and the close contact with many lives may teach to the poetic nature lessons of courage, of self-suppression, of resolute goodwill, and may transform into an added dignity the tumult of emotions which might else have run riot in his heart. Yet it is less often from moods of self-control than from moods of self-abandonment that the fount of poetry springs; and herein it was that Wordsworth's especial felicity lay—that there was no one feeling in him which the world had either repressed or tainted; that he had no joy which might not be the harmless joy of all; and that therefore it was when he was most unreservedly himself that he was most profoundly human. All that was needful for him was to strike down into the deep of his heart. Or, using his own words, we may compare his tranquil existence to

A crystal river,
Diaphanous because it travels slowly,

and in which poetic thoughts rose unimpeded to the surface, like bubbles through the pellucid stream.

The first hint of many of his briefer poems is to be found in his sister's diary :

"April 15, 1802. When we were in the woods below Gowbarrow Park we saw a few *daffodils* close to the water side. As we went along there were more, and yet more; and at last, under the boughs of the trees, we saw there was a long belt of them along the shore. I never saw daffodils so beautiful. They grew among the mossy stones about them; some rested their heads on the stones as on a pillow; the rest tossed, and reeled, and danced, and seemed as if they verily danced with the wind, they looked so gay and glancing."

"July 30, 1802. Left London between five and six o'clock of the morning, outside the Dover coach. A beautiful morning. The city, St. Paul's, with the river, a multitude of little boats, made a beautiful sight as we crossed Westminster Bridge; the houses not overhung by their clouds of smoke, were spread out endlessly; yet the sun shone so brightly, with such a pure light, that there was something like the purity of one of Nature's own grand spectacles. Arrived at Calais at four in the morning of July 31st. Delightful walks in the evenings, seeing far off in the west the coast of England like a cloud, crested with Dover Castle, the evening star, and the glory of the sky. The reflections in the water were more beautiful than the sky itself; purple waves brighter than precious stones for ever melting away upon the sands."

How simple are the elements of these delights! There is nothing here, except fraternal affection, a sunrise, a sunset, a flock of bright wild flowers; and yet the sonnets on *Westminster Bridge* and *Calais Sands*, and the stanzas on the *Daffodils*, have taken their place among the permanent records of the profoundest human joy.

Another tour,—this time through Scotland,—undertaken in August 1803, inspired Wordsworth with several of his best pieces. Miss Wordsworth's diary of this tour has been lately published, and should be familiar to all lovers of Nature. The sister's journal is indeed the best introduction to the brother's poems. It has not—it cannot have—their dignity and beauty; but it exemplifies the same method of regarding Nature, the same self-identification with her subtler aspects and entrance into her profounder charm. It is interesting to notice how the same impression strikes both minds at once. From the sister's it is quickly reflected in words of exquisite delicacy and simplicity; in the brother's it germinates, and reappears.

it may be months or years afterwards, as the nucleus of a
mass of thought and feeling which has grown round it in
his musing soul.   The travellers' encounter with two Highland girls on the shore of Loch Lomond is a good instance
of this.   "One of the girls," writes Miss Wordsworth,
"was exceedingly beautiful; and the figures of both of
them, in grey plaids falling to their feet, their faces only
being uncovered, excited our attention before we spoke to
them; but they answered us so sweetly that we were quite
delighted, at the same time that they stared at us with an
innocent look of wonder.   I think I never heard the
English language sound more sweetly than from the mouth
of the elder of these girls, while she stood at the gate
answering our inquiries, her face flushed with the rain;
her pronunciation was clear and distinct, without difficulty, yet slow, as if like a foreign speech."

> A face with gladness overspread!
> Soft smiles, by human kindness bred!
> And seemliness complete, that sways
> Thy courtesies, about thee plays;
> With no restraint, but such as springs
> From quick and eager visitings
> Of thoughts that lie beyond the reach
> Of thy few words of English speech:
> A bondage sweetly brooked, a strife
> That gives thy gestures grace and life!
> So have I, not unmoved in mind,
> Seen birds of tempest-loving kind
> Thus beating up against the wind.

The travellers saw more of this girl, and Miss Wordsworth's opinion was confirmed.   But to Wordsworth his
glimpse of her became a veritable romance.   He commemorated it in his poem of *The Highland Girl*, soon after
his return from Scotland; he narrated it once more in his

poem of *The Three Cottage Girls*, written nearly twenty
years afterwards ; and "the sort of prophecy," he says in
1843, "with which the verses conclude, has, through
God's goodness, been realized ; and now, approaching the
close of my seventy-third year, I have a most vivid remembrance of her, and the beautiful objects with which she
was surrounded." Nay, more ; he has elsewhere informed
us, with some naïveté, that the first few lines of his
exquisite poem to his wife, *She was a phantom of delight*,
were originally composed as a description of this Highland
maid, who would seem almost to have formed for him ever
afterwards a kind of type and image of loveliness.

That such a meeting as this should have formed so long-
remembered an incident in the poet's life will appear,
perhaps, equally ridiculous to the philosopher and to the
man of the world. The one would have given less, the
other would have demanded more. And yet the quest of
beauty, like the quest of truth, reaps its surest reward
when it is disinterested as well as keen ; and the true lover
of human-kind will often draw his most exquisite
moments from what to most men seems but the shadow of
a joy. Especially, as in this case, his heart will be pro-
digal of the impulses of that protecting tenderness which
it is the blessing of early girlhood to draw forth unwit-
tingly, and to enjoy unknown,—affections which lead to no
declaration, and desire no return ; which are the spontaneous effluence of the very Spirit of Love in man ; and
which play and hover around winning innocence like the
coruscations round the head of the unconscious Iulus, a
soft and unconsuming flame.

It was well, perhaps, that Wordsworth's romance should
come to him in this remote and fleeting fashion. For
to the Priest of Nature it was fitting that all things

else should be harmonious, indeed, but accessory; that
joy should not be so keen, nor sorrow so desolating, nor
love itself so wildly strong, as to prevent him from going
out upon the mountains with a heart at peace, and receiving "in a wise passiveness" the voices of earth and
heaven.

CHAPTER VI.

THE year 1803 saw the beginning of a friendship which formed a valuable element in Wordsworth's life. Sir George Beaumont, of Coleorton Hall, Essex, a descendant of the dramatist, and representative of a family long distinguished for talent and culture, was staying with Coleridge at Greta Hall, Keswick, when, hearing of Coleridge's affection for Wordsworth, he was struck with the wish to bring Wordsworth also to Keswick, and bought and presented to him a beautiful piece of land at Applethwaite, under Skiddaw, in the hope that he might be induced to settle there. Coleridge was soon afterwards obliged to leave England in search of health, and the plan fell through. A characteristic letter of Wordsworth's records his feelings on the occasion. "Dear Sir George," he writes, "if any person were to be informed of the particulars of your kindness to me, if it were described to him in all its delicacy and nobleness, and he should afterwards be told that I suffered eight weeks to elapse without writing to you one word of thanks or acknowledgment, he would deem it a thing absolutely *impossible*. It is nevertheless true.

"Owing to a set of painful and uneasy sensations

F

which I have, more or less, at all times about my chest, I
deferred writing to you, being at first made still more
uncomfortable by travelling, and loathing to do violence to
myself in what ought to be an act of pure pleasure and
enjoyment, viz. the expression of my deep sense of your
goodness. This feeling was indeed so strong in me, as to
make me look upon the act of writing to you as a thing
not to be done but in my best, my purest, and my happiest
moments. Many of these I had, but then I had not my
pen, ink, and paper before me, my conveniences, 'my appli-
ances and means to boot;' all which, the moment that I
thought of them, seemed to disturb and impair the
sanctity of my pleasure. I contented myself with thinking over my complacent feelings, and breathing forth
solitary gratulations and thanksgivings, which I did in
many a sweet and many a wild place, during my late
tour."

The friendship of which this act of delicate generosity
was the beginning was maintained till Sir George Beaumont's death in 1827, and formed for many years Wordsworth's closest link with the world of art and culture.
Sir George was himself a painter as well as a connoisseur,
and his landscapes are not without indications of the
strong feeling for nature which he undoubtedly possessed.
Wordsworth, who had seen very few pictures, but was a
penetrating critic of those which he knew, discerned this
vein of true feeling in his friend's work, and has idealized
a small landscape which Sir George had given him, in a
sonnet which reproduces the sense of happy pause and
voluntary fixation with which the mind throws itself into
some scene where Art has given

> To one brief moment caught from fleeting time
> The appropriate calm of blest eternity.

There was another pursuit in which Sir George Beaumont was much interested, and in which painter and poet were well fitted to unite. The landscape-gardener, as Wordsworth says, should "work in the spirit of Nature, with an invisible hand of art." And he shows how any real success can only be achieved when the designer is willing to incorporate himself with the scenery around him ; to postpone to its indications the promptings of his own pride or caprice ; to interpret Nature to herself by completing touches ; to correct her with deference, and as it were to caress her without importunity. And rising to that aspect of the question which connects it with human society, he is strenuous in condemnation of that taste, not so much for solitude as for isolation, which can tolerate no neighbourhood, and finds its only enjoyment in the sense of monopoly.

"Laying out grounds, as it is called, may be considered as a liberal art, in some sort like poetry and painting; its object ought to be to move the affections under the control of good sense; and surely the affections of those who have the deepest perception of the beauty of Nature,—who have the most valuable feelings, that is the most permanent, the most independent, the most ennobling, connected with Nature and human life. No liberal art aims merely at the gratification of an individual or a class; the painter or poet is degraded in proportion as he does so. The true servants of the arts pay homage to the human kind as impersonated in unwarped and enlightened minds. If this be so when we are merely putting together words or colours, how much more ought the feeling to prevail when we are in the midst of the realities of things; of the beauty and harmony, of the joy and happiness, of loving creatures; of men and children, of birds and beasts, of hills and streams, and trees and flowers; with the changes of night and day, evening and morning, summer and winter; and all their unwearied actions and energies, as benign in the spirit that animates them

as they are beautiful and grand in that form of clothing which
is given to them for the delight of our senses! What then
shall we say of many great mansions, with their unqualified
expulsion of human creatures from their neighbourhood,
happy or not; houses which do what is fabled of the upas
tree—breathe out death and desolation! For my part, strip
my neighbourhood of human beings, and I should think it
one of the greatest privations I could undergo. You have
all the poverty of solitude, nothing of its elevation."

This passage is from a letter of Wordsworth's to Sir
George Beaumont, who was engaged at the time in re-
building and laying out Coleorton. The poet himself
planned and superintended some of these improvements,
and wrote for various points of interest in the grounds
inscriptions which form dignified examples of that kind
of composition.

Nor was Sir George Beaumont the only friend whom
the poet's taste assisted in the choice of a site or the disposition of pleasure-grounds. More than one seat in the
Lake-country—among them one home of pre-eminent
beauty—have owed to Wordsworth no small part of their
ordered charm. In this way, too, the poet is with us still;
his presence has a strange reality as we look on some
majestic prospect of interwinding lake and mountain
which his design has made more beautifully visible to the
children's children of those he loved; as we stand, perhaps, in some shadowed garden-ground where his will has
had its way,—has framed Helvellyn's far-off summit in
an arch of tossing green, and embayed in towering forest-
trees the long lawns of a silent Valley,—fit haunt for lofty
aspiration and for brooding calm.

But of all woodland ways which Wordsworth's skill
designed or his feet frequented, not one was dearer to him,

(if I may pass thus by a gentle transition to another of
the strong affections of his life), than a narrow path
through a firwood near his cottage, which " was known
to the poet's household by the name of John's Grove."
For in the year 1800 his brother, John Wordsworth, a
few years younger than himself, and captain of an East
Indiaman, had spent eight months in the poet's cottage at
Grasmere. The two brothers had seen little of each
other since childhood, and the poet had now the delight
of discovering in the sailor a character congenial to his
own, and an appreciation of poetry—and of the *Lyrical
Ballads* especially—which was intense and delicate in an
unusual degree. In both brothers, too, there was the
same love of nature ; and after John's departure, the poet
pleased himself with imagining the visions of Grasmere
which beguiled the watches of many a night at sea, or
with tracing the pathway which the sailor's instinct had
planned and trodden amid trees so thickly planted as to
baffle a less practised skill. John Wordsworth, on the
other hand, looked forward to Grasmere as the final goal
of his wanderings, and intended to use his own savings
to set the poet free from worldly cares.

Two more voyages the sailor made with such hopes as
these, and amid a frequent interchange of books and
letters with his brother at home.   Then, in February
1805, he set sail from Portsmouth, in command of the
"Abergavenny" East Indiaman, bound for India and China.
Through the incompetence of the pilot who was taking
her out of the Channel, the ship struck on the Shambles
off the Bill of Portland, on February 5, 1805.   "She
struck," says Wordsworth, "at 5 p.m.   Guns were fired
immediately, and were continued to be fired.   She was
gotten off the rock at half-past seven, but had taken in

so much water, in spite of constant pumping, as to be
water-logged. They had, however, hope that she might
still be run upon Weymouth sands, and with this view
continued pumping and baling till eleven, when she
went down. . . . . A few minutes before the ship went
down my brother was seen talking to the first mate, with
apparent cheerfulness; and he was standing on the hen-
coop, which is the point from which he could overlook
the whole ship, the moment she went down—dying, as he
had lived, in the very place and point where his duty
stationed him."

"For myself," he continues elsewhere, "I feel that
there is something cut out of my life which cannot be
restored. I never thought of him but with hope and
delight. We looked forward to the time, not distant, as
we thought, when he would settle near us—when the
task of his life would be over, and he would have nothing
to do but reap his reward. By that time I hoped also
that the chief part of my labours would be executed, and
that I should be able to show him that he had not placed
a false confidence in me. I never wrote a line without a
thought of giving him pleasure; my writings, printed
and manuscript, were his delight, and one of the chief
solaces of his long voyages. But let me stop. I will not
be cast down; were it only for his sake I will not be
dejected. I have much yet to do, and pray God to give me
strength and power: his part of the agreement between us
is brought to an end, mine continues ; and I hope when I
shall be able to think of him with a calmer mind, that
the remembrance of him dead will even animate me more
than the joy which I had in him living."

In these and the following reflections there is nothing
of novelty; yet there is an interest in the spectacle of

this strong and simple mind confronted with the universal problems, and taking refuge in the thoughts which have satisfied, or scarcely satisfied, so many generations of mourning men.

"A thousand times have I asked myself, as your tender sympathy led me to do, 'Why was he taken away?' and I have answered the question as you have done. In fact there is no other answer which can satisfy, and lay the mind at rest. Why have we a choice, and a will, and a notion of justice and injustice, enabling us to be moral agents? Why have we sympathies that make the best of us so afraid of inflicting pain and sorrow, which yet we see dealt about so lavishly by the Supreme Governor? Why should our notions of right towards each other, and to all sentient beings within our influence, differ so widely from what appears to be His notion and rule, *if every thing were to end here?* Would it not be blasphemy to say that, upon the supposition of the thinking principle being *destroyed by death*, however inferior we may be to the great Cause and Ruler of things we have *more of love* in our nature than He has? The thought is monstrous; and yet how to get rid of it, except upon the supposition of *another* and a *better world*, I do not see."

From this calamity, as from all the lessons of life, Wordsworth drew all the benefit which it was empowered to bring. "A deep distress hath humanized my soul,"— what lover of poetry does not know the pathetic lines in which he bears witness to the teaching of sorrow? Other griefs, too, he had—the loss of two children in 1812; his sister's chronic illness, beginning in 1832; his daughter's death in 1847. All these he felt to the full; and yet, until his daughter's death, which was more than his failing energies could bear, these bereavements were but the

thinly-scattered clouds "in a great sea of blue"—seasons
of mourning here and there among years which never lost
their hold on peace; which knew no shame and no re-
morse, no desolation and no fear; whose days were never
long with weariness, nor their nights broken at the touch
of woe. Even when we speak of his tribulations, it is his
happiness which rises in our minds.

And inasmuch as this felicity is the great fact of
Wordsworth's life—since his history is for the most part
but the history of a halycon calm—we find ourselves
forced upon the question whether such a life is to be
held desirable or no. Happiness with honour was the
ideal of Solon; is it also ours? To the modern spirit,—
to the Christian, in whose ears counsels of perfection have
left "a presence that is not to be put by," this question,
at which a Greek would have smiled, is of no such easy
solution.

To us, perhaps, in computing the fortune of any one
whom we hold dear, it may seem more needful to inquire
not whether he has had enough of joy, but whether he
has had enough of sorrow; whether the blows of circumstance have wholly shaped his character from the rock;
whether his soul has taken lustre and purity in the re-
finer's fire. Nor is it only (as some might say) for violent
and faulty natures that sorrow is the best. It is true
that by sorrow only can the headstrong and presumptuous
spirit be shamed into gentleness and solemnized into
humility. But sorrow is used also by the Power above
us in cases where we men would have shrunk in horror
from so rough a touch. Natures that were already of a
heroic unselfishness, of a childlike purity, have been
raised ere now by anguish upon anguish, woe after woe,
to a height of holiness which we may believe that they

could have reached by no other road. Why should it not
be so? since there is no limit to the soul's possible elevation, why should her purifying trials have any assignable
end? She is of a metal which can grow for ever brighter
in the fiercening flame. And if, then, we would still pro-
nounce the true Beatitudes not on the rejoicing, the satisfied, the highly-honoured, but after an ancient and sterner
pattern, what account are we to give of Wordsworth's
long years of blissful calm?

In the first place, we may say that his happiness was
as wholly free from vulgar or transitory elements as a
man's can be. It lay in a life which most men would
have found austere and blank indeed; a life from which
not Crœsus only, but Solon would have turned in scorn,
a life of poverty and retirement, of long apparent failure,
and honour that came tardily at the close; it was a happiness nourished on no sacrifice of other men, on no eager
appropriation of the goods of earth, but springing from
a single eye and a loving spirit, and wrought from those
primary emotions which are the innocent birthright of all.
And if it be answered that however truly philosophic,
however sacredly pure, his happiness may have been, yet
its wisdom and its holiness were without an effort, and,
that it is effort which makes the philosopher and the
saint : then we must use in answer his own Platonic
scheme of things, to express a thought which we can but
dimly apprehend; and we must say that though progress
be inevitably linked in our minds with struggle, yet
neither do we conceive of struggle as without a pause;
there must be prospect-places in the long ascent of souls ;
and the whole of this earthly life—this one existence,
standing we know not where among the myriad that have
been for us or shall be—may not be too much to occupy

with one of those outlooks of vision and of prophecy,
when

> In a season of calm weather
> Though inland far we be,
> Our souls have sight of that immortal sea
> Which brought us hither ;
> Can in a moment travel thither,
> And see the children sport upon the shore,
> And hear the mighty waters rolling evermore.

CHAPTER VII.

THE year 1805, which bereft Wordsworth of a beloved brother, brought with it also another death, which was felt by the whole English nation like a private calamity. The emotion which Wordsworth felt at the news of Trafalgar,—the way in which he managed to intertwine the memories of Nelson and of his own brother in his heart,—may remind us fitly at this point of our story of the distress and perplexity of nations which for so many years surrounded the quiet Grasmere home, and of the strong responsive emotion with which the poet met each shock of European fates.

When England first took up arms against the French revolution, Wordsworth's feeling, as we have seen, had been one of unmixed sorrow and shame. Bloody and terrible as the revolution had become, it was still in some sort representative of human freedom; at any rate it might still seem to contain possibilities of progress such as the retrograde despotisms with which England allied herself could never know. But the conditions of the contest changed before long. France had not the wisdom, the courage, the constancy to play to the end the part for which she had seemed chosen among the nations. It was her conduct towards Switzerland which decisively altered

Wordsworth's view. He saw her valiant spirit of self-
defence corrupted into lust of glory; her eagerness for the
abolition of unjust privilege turned into a contentment
with equality of degradation under a despot's heel.
"One man, of men the meanest too,"—for such the First
Consul must needs appear to the moralist's eye,—was

> Raised up to sway the world—to do, undo;
> With mighty nations for his underlings.

And history herself seemed vulgarized by the repetition of
her ancient tales of war and overthrow on a scale of such
apparent magnitude, but with no glamour of distance to
hide the baseness of the agencies by which the destinies
of Europe were shaped anew. This was an occasion
that tried the hearts of men; it was not easy to remain
through all those years at once undazzled and untempted,
and never in the blackest hour to despair of human
virtue.

In his tract on *The Convention of Cintra*, 1808, Wordsworth has given the fullest expression to this undaunted
temper :—

"Oppression, its own blind and predestined enemy, has poured
this of blessedness upon Spain—that the enormity of the outrages
of which she has been the victim has created an object of love
and of hatred, of apprehensions and of wishes, adequate (if
that be possible) to the utmost demands of the human spirit.
The heart that serves in this cause, if it languish, must
languish from its own constitutional weakness, and not through
want of nourishment from without. But it is a belief pro-
pagated in books, and which passes currently among talking
men as part of their familiar wisdom, that the hearts of the
many *are* constitutionally weak, that they *do* languish, and
are slow to answer to the requisitions of things. I entreat
those who are in this delusion to look behind them and

about them for the evidence of experience. Now this, rightly
understood, not only gives no support to any such belief,
but proves that the truth is in direct opposition to it. The
history of all ages—tumults after tumults, wars foreign or
civil, with short or with no breathing-places from generation to
generation ; the senseless weaving and interweaving of factions,
vanishing, and reviving, and piercing each other like the
Northern Lights ; public commotions, and those in the breast
of the individual ; the long calenture to which the Lover is subject ; the blast, like the blast of the desert, which sweeps peren-
nially through a frightful solitude of its own making in the
mind of the Gamester ; the slowly quickening, but ever quickening, descent of appetite down which the Miser is propelled ; the
agony and cleaving oppression of grief ; the ghost-like hauntings
of shame ; the incubus of revenge ; the life-distemper of ambition . . . these demonstrate incontestably that the passions of
men, (I mean the soul of sensibility in the heart of man), in all
quarrels, in all contests, in all quests, in all delights, in all
employments which are either sought by men or thrust upon
them, do immeasurably transcend their objects. The true
sorrow of humanity consists in this—not that the mind of
man fails, but that the cause and demands of action and of
life so rarely correspond with the dignity and intensity of
human desires ; and hence, that which is slow to languish is too
easily turned aside and abused. But, with the remembrance of
what has been done, and in the face of the interminable evils
which are threatened, a Spaniard can never have cause to com-
plain of this while a follower of the tyrant remains in arms
upon the Peninsula."

It was passages such as this, perhaps, which led Can-
ning to declare that Wordsworth's pamphlet was the
finest piece of political eloquence which had appeared
since Burke. And yet if we compare it with Burke, or
with the great Greek exemplar of all those who would
give speech the cogency of act,—we see at once the
causes of its practical failure. In Demosthenes the

thoughts and principles are often as lofty as any patriot
can express; but their loftiness, in his speech, as in the
very truth of things, seemed but to add to their immediate reality. They were beaten and inwoven into the
facts of the hour; action seemed to turn on them as on
its only possible pivot; it was as though Virtue and
Freedom hung armed in heaven above the assembly, and
in the visible likeness of immortal ancestors beckoned
upon an urgent way. Wordsworth's mood of mind, on the
other hand, as he has depicted it in two sonnets written
at the same time as his tract, explains why it was that
that appeal was rather a solemn protest than an effective
exhortation. In the first sonnet he describes the surroundings of his task,—the dark wood and rocky cave,
"the hollow vale which foaming torrents fill with omni-
present murmur :"—

> Here mighty Nature! in this school sublime
> I weigh the hopes and fears of suffering Spain;
> For her consult the auguries of time,
> And through the human heart explore my way,
> And look and listen, gathering whence I may
> Triumph, and thoughts no bondage can restrain.

And then he proceeds to conjecture what effect his tract
will produce :—

> I dropped my pen, and listened to the wind,
> That sang of trees uptorn and vessels tost;
> A midnight harmony, and wholly lost
> To the general sense of men, by chains confined
> Of business, care, or pleasure,—or resigned
> To timely sleep. Thought I, the impassioned strain
> Which without aid of numbers I sustain
> Like acceptation from the world will find.

This deliberate and lonely emotion was fitter to inspire

grave poetry than a pamphlet appealing to an immediate
crisis. And the sonnets dedicated *To Liberty* (1802-16)
are the outcome of many moods like these.

It is little to say of these sonnets that they are the
most permanent record in our literature of the Napoleonic
war. For that distinction they have few competitors.
Two magnificent songs of Campbell's, an ode of Coleridge's,
a few spirited stanzas of Byron's—strangely enough
there is little besides these that lives in the national
memory, till we come to the ode which summed up the
long contest a generation later, when its great captain
passed away. But these *Sonnets to Liberty* are worthy
of comparison with the noblest passages of patriotic verse
or prose whïch all our history has inspired—the passages
where Shakespeare brings his rays to focus on " this earth,
this realm, this England,"—or where the dread of national
dishonour has kindled Chatham to an iron glow,—or
where Milton rises from the polemic into the prophet,
and Burke from the partisan into the philosopher. The
armoury of Wordsworth, indeed, was not forged with the
same fire as that of these "invincible knights of old." He
had not swayed senates, nor directed policies, nor gathered
into one ardent bosom all the spirit of a heroic age. But
he had deeply felt what it is that makes the greatness of
nations ; in that extremity no man was more staunch than
he ; no man more unwaveringly disdained unrighteous
empire, or kept the might of moral forces more stead-
fastly in view. Not Stein could place a manlier reliance
on "a few strong instincts and a few plain rules ;" not
Fichte could invoke more convincingly the " great allies"
which work with " Man's unconquerable mind."

Here and there, indeed, throughout these sonnets are
scattered strokes of high poetic admiration or scorn which

could hardly be overmatched in Æschylus. Such is the
indignant correction—

> Call not the royal Swede unfortunate,
> Who never did to Fortune bend the knee!

or the stern touch which closes a description of Flami-
ninus' proclamation at the Isthmian games, according
liberty to Greece,—

> A gift of that which is not to be given
> By all the blended powers of Earth and Heaven!

Space forbids me to dwell in detail on these noble
poems,—on the well-known sonnets to Venice, to Milton,
&c. ; on the generous tributes to the heroes of the contest,—Schill, Hoffer, Toussaint, Palafox ; or on the
series which contrast the instinctive greatness of the
Spanish people at bay, with Napoleon's lying promises
and inhuman pride. But if Napoleon's career afforded to
Wordsworth a poetic example, impressive as that of Xerxes
to the Greeks, of lawless and intoxicated power, there was
need of some contrasted figure more notable than Hoffer
or Palafox from which to draw the lessons which great
contests can teach of unselfish valour. Was there then
any man, by land or sea, who might serve as the poet's
type of the ideal hero ? To an Englishman, at least, this
question carries its own reply. For by a singular destiny
England, with a thousand years of noble history behind
her, has chosen for her best-loved, for her national hero,
not an Arminius from the age of legend, not a Henri
Quatre from the age of chivalry, but a man whom men
still living have seen and known. For indeed England
and all the world as to this man were of one accord ;
and when in victory, on his ship *Victory*, Nelson passed

away, the thrill which shook mankind was of a nature such as perhaps was never felt at any other death,—so unanimous was the feeling of friends and foes that earth had lost her crowning example of impassioned self-devotedness and of heroic honour.

And yet it might have seemed that between Nelson's nature and Wordsworth's there was little in common. The obvious limitations of the great Admiral's culture and character were likely to be strongly felt by the philosophic poet. And a serious crime, of which Nelson was commonly, though, as now appears, erroneously,[1] supposed to be guilty, was sure to be judged by Wordsworth with great severity.

Wordsworth was, in fact, hampered by some such feelings of disapproval. He even tells us, with that naive affectionateness which often makes us smile, that he has had recourse to the character of his own brother John for the qualities in which the great Admiral appeared to him to have been deficient. But on these hesitations it would be unjust to dwell. I mention them only to bring out the fact that between these two men, so different in outward fates,—between "the adored, the incomparable Nelson" and the homely poet, "retired as noontide dew,"— there was a moral likeness so profound that the ideal of the recluse was realized in the public life of the hero, and, on the other hand, the hero himself is only seen as completely heroic when his impetuous life stands out for us from the solemn background of the poet's calm. And surely these two natures taken together make the perfect Englishman. Nor is there any portrait fitter than that of

[1] The researches of Sir Nicholas Nicolas, (*Letters and Despatches of Lord Nelson*, vol. vii. Appendix), have placed Lord Nelson's connexion with Lady Hamilton in an unexpected light.

The Happy Warrior to go forth to all lands as representing the English character at its height—a figure not
ill-matching with " Plutarch's men."

For indeed this short poem is in itself a manual of
greatness ; there is a Roman majesty in its simple and
weighty speech. And what eulogy was ever nobler than
that passage where, without definite allusion or quoted
name, the poet depicts, as it were, the very summit of
glory in the well-remembered aspect of the Admiral in his
last and greatest hour ?

> Whose powers shed round him, in the common strife,
> Or mild concerns of ordinary life,
> A constant influence, a peculiar grace ;
> But who, if he be called upon to face
> Some awful moment to which Heaven has joined
> Great issues, good or bad for human kind,
> *Is happy as a Lover, and attired*
> *With sudden brightness, like a Man inspired.*

Or again, where the hidden thought of Nelson's womanly
tenderness, of his constant craving for the green earth and
home affections in the midst of storm and war. melts the
stern verses into a sudden change of tone :—

> He who, though thus endued as with a sense
> And faculty for storm and turbulence,
> *Is yet a Soul whose master-bias leans*
> *To homefelt pleasures and to gentle scenes ;*
> Sweet images ! which, wheresoe'er he be,
> Are at his heart ; and such fidelity
> It is his darling passion to approve ;—
> More brave for this, that he hath much to love.

Compare with this the end of the *Song at Brougham
Castle*, where, at the words " alas ! the fervent harper did
not know—" the strain changes from the very spirit of
chivalry to the gentleness of Nature's calm. Nothing

can be more characteristic of Wordsworth than contrasts
like this.   They teach us to remember that his accustomed
mildness is the fruit of no indolent or sentimental peace ;
and that, on the other hand, when his counsels are sternest,
and "his voice is still for war," this is no voice of hard-
ness or of vainglory, but the reluctant resolution of a heart
which fain would yield itself to other energies, and have
no message but of love.

There is one more point in which the character of
Nelson has fallen in with one of the lessons which Wordsworth is never tired of enforcing, the lesson that virtue
grows by the strenuousness of its exercise, that it gains
strength as it wrestles with pain and difficulty, and con-
verts the shocks of circumstance into an energy of its
proper glow.   The Happy Warrior is one,

> Who, doomed to go in company with Pain,
> And Fear, and Bloodshed, miserable train !
> Turns his necessity to glorious gain ;
> In face of these doth exercise a power
> Which is our human nature's highest dower ;
> Controls them and subdues, transmutes, bereaves
> Of their bad influence, and their good receives ;
> By objects which might force the soul to abate
> Her feeling, rendered more compassionate ;—

and so further, in words which recall the womanly tenderness, the almost exaggerated feeling for others' pain,
which showed itself memorably in face of the blazing
Orient, and in the harbour at Teneriffe, and in the cock-
pit at Trafalgar.

In such lessons as these,—such lessons as *The Happy
Warrior* or the Patriotic Sonnets teach,—there is, of course,
little that is absolutely novel.   We were already aware
that the ideal hero should be as gentle as he is brave, that

he should act always from the highest motives, nor greatly
care for any reward save the consciousness of having done
his duty. We were aware that the true strength of a
nation is moral and not material; that dominion which
rests on mere military force is destined quickly to decay;
that the tyrant, however admired and prosperous, is in
reality despicable, and miserable, and alone; that the true
man should face death itself rather than parley with dishonour. These truths are *admitted* in all ages; yet it is
scarcely stretching language to say that they are *known* to
but few men. Or at least, though in a great nation there
be many who will act on them instinctively, and approve
them by a self-surrendering faith, there are few who can
so put them forth in speech as to bring them home with
a fresh conviction and an added glow; who can sum up,
like Æschylus, the contrast between Hellenic freedom and
barbarian despotism in "one trump's peal that set all
Greeks aflame;" can thrill, like Virgil, a world-wide
empire with the recital of the august simplicities of early
Rome.

To those who would know these things with a vital
knowledge—a conviction which would remain unshaken
were the whole world in arms for wrong—it is before all
things necessary to strengthen the inner monitions by the
companionship of these noble souls. And if a poet, by
strong concentration of thought, by striving in all things
along the upward way, can leave us in a few pages as it
were a summary of patriotism, a manual of national
honour, he surely has his place among his country's bene-
factors not only by that kind of courtesy which the
nation extends to men of letters of whom her masses take
little heed, but with a title as assured as any warrior or
statesman, and with no less direct a claim.

CHAPTER VIII.

CHILDREN—LIFE AT RYDAL MOUNT—" THE EXCURSION."

IT may be well at this point to return to the quiet chronicle of the poet's life at Grasmere; where his cottage was becoming too small for an increasing family. His eldest son, John, was born in 1803; his eldest daughter, Dorothy or Dora, in 1804. Then came Thomas, born 1806; and Catherine, born 1808; and the list is ended by William, born 1810, and now (1880) the only survivor. In the spring of 1808 Wordsworth left Townend for Allan Bank,—a more roomy, but an uncomfortable house, at the north end of Grasmere. From thence he removed for a time, in 1811, to the Parsonage at Grasmere.

Wordsworth was the most affectionate of fathers; and allusions to his children occur frequently in his poetry. Dora—who was the delight of his later years—has been described at length in *The Triad*. Shorter and simpler, but more completely successful, is the picture of Catherine in the little poem which begins "Loving she is, and tractable, though wild," with its homely simile for childhood—its own existence sufficient to fill it with gladness :

> As a faggot sparkles on the hearth
> Not less if unattended and alone
> Than when both young and old sit gathered round
> And take delight in its activity.

The next notice of this beloved child is in the sonnet, "Surprised by joy, impatient as the wind," written when she had already been removed from his side. She died in 1812, and was closely followed by her brother Thomas. Wordsworth's grief for these children was profound, violent, and lasting, to an extent which those who imagine him as not only calm but passionless might have some difficulty in believing. "Referring once," says his friend Mr. Aubrey de Vere, "to two young children of his who had died about *forty years* previously, he described the details of their illnesses with an exactness and an impetuosity of troubled excitement, such as might have been expected if the bereavement had taken place but a few weeks before. The lapse of time seemed to have left the sorrow submerged indeed, but still in all its first freshness. Yet I afterwards heard that at the time of the illness, at least in the case of one of the two children, it was impossible to rouse his attention to the danger. He chanced to be then under the immediate spell of one of those fits of poetic inspiration which descended on him like a cloud. Till the cloud had drifted, he could see nothing beyond."

This anecdote illustrates the fact, which to those who knew Wordsworth well was sufficiently obvious, that the characteristic calm of his writings was the result of no coldness of temperament but of a deliberate philosophy. The pregnant force of his language in dealing with those dearest to him—his wife, his sister, his brother—is proof enough of this. The frequent allusions in his correspondence to the physical exhaustion brought on by the act of poetical composition indicate a frame which, though made robust by exercise and temperance, was by nature excitable rather than strong. And even in the direction in which we should least have expected it, there is reason

to believe that there were capacities of feeling in him
which never broke from his control. "Had I been a
writer of love-poetry," he is reported to have said, "it
would have been natural to me to write it with a degree
of warmth which could hardly have been approved by
my principles, and which might have been undesirable
for the reader."

Wordsworth's paternal feelings, at any rate, were, as
has been said, exceptionally strong ; and the impossibility
of remaining in a house filled with sorrowful memories
rendered him doubly anxious to obtain a permanent home.
"The house which I have for some time occupied," he
writes to Lord Lonsdale, in January 1813, "is the Parsonage of Grasmere. It stands close by the churchyard, and I
have found it absolutely necessary that we should quit a
place which, by recalling to our minds at every moment
the losses we have sustained in the course of the last
year, would grievously retard our progress towards that
tranquillity which it is our duty to aim at." It happened
that Rydal Mount became vacant at this moment, and
in the spring of 1813 the Wordsworths migrated to this
their favourite and last abode.

Rydal Mount has probably been oftener described than
any other English poet's home since Shakespeare; and
few homes, certainly, have been moulded into such close
accordance with their inmates' nature. The house, which
has been altered since Wordsworth's day, stands looking
southward, on the rocky side of Nab Scar, above Rydal
Lake. The garden was described by Bishop Wordsworth
immediately after his uncle's death, while every terrace-
walk and flowering alley spoke of the poet's loving care.
He tells of the "tall ash-tree, in which a thrush has
sung, for hours together, during many years ; " of the

"laburnum in which the osier cage of the doves was hung;" of the stone steps "in the interstices of which grow the yellow flowering poppy, and the wild geranium or Poor Robin,"—

Gay
With his red stalks upon a sunny day.

And then of the terraces—one levelled for Miss Fenwick's use, and welcome to himself in aged years ; and one ascending, and leading to the "far terrace" on the mountain's side, where the poet was wont to murmur his verses as they came. Within the house were disposed his simple treasures : the ancestral almery, on which the names of unknown Wordsworths may be deciphered still; Sir George Beaumont's pictures of "The White Doe of Rylstone" and "The Thorn," and the cuckoo clock which brought vernal thoughts to cheer the sleepless bed of age, and which sounded its noonday summons when his spirit fled.

Wordsworth's worldly fortunes, as if by some benignant guardianship of Providence, were at all times proportioned to his successive needs. About the date of his removal to Rydal (in March 1813) he was appointed, through Lord Lonsdale's interest, to the distributorship of stamps for the county of Westmoreland, to which office the same post for Cumberland was afterwards added. He held this post till August 1842, when he resigned it without a retiring pension, and it was conferred on his second son. He was allowed to reside at Rydal, which was counted as a suburb of Ambleside ; and as the duties of the place were light, and mainly performed by a most competent and devoted clerk, there was no drawback to the advantage of an increase of income which released him from anxiety as to the future. A more lucrative office—the collectorship of Whitehaven—was subsequently offered to him ;

but he declined it, "nor would exchange his Sabine valley
for riches and a load of care."

Though Wordsworth's life at Rydal was a retired
one, it was not that of a recluse. As years went on he
became more and more recognized as a centre of spiritual
strength and illumination, and was sought not only by
those who were already his neighbours, but by some who
became so mainly for his sake. Southey at Keswick was
a valued friend, though Wordsworth did not greatly
esteem him as a poet. De Quincey, originally attracted
to the district by admiration for Wordsworth, remained
there for many years, and poured forth a criticism strangely
compounded of the utterances of the hero-worshipper and
the *valet-de-chambre.* Professor Wilson, of the *Noctes Am-
brosianæ,* never showed, perhaps, to so much advantage as
when he walked by the side of the master whose greatness
he was one of the first to detect. Dr. Arnold of Rugby
made the neighbouring home at Fox How a focus of warm
affections and of intellectual life. And Hartley Coleridge,
whose fairy childhood had inspired one of Wordsworth's
happiest pieces, continued to lead among the dales of
Westmoreland a life which showed how much of genius
and goodness a single weakness can nullify.

Other friends there were, too, less known to fame, but
of exceptional powers of appreciation and sympathy. The
names of Mrs. Fletcher and her daughters, Lady Richardson and Mrs. Davy, should not be omitted in any record
of the poet's life at Rydal. And many humbler neighbours may be recognized in the characters of the *Excursion*
and other poems. The *Wanderer,* indeed, is a picture of
Wordsworth himself—" an idea," as he says, " of what I
fancied my own character might have become in his circumstances." But the *Solitary* was suggested by a broken man

who took refuge in Grasmere from the world in which he
had found no peace; and the characters described as
lying in the churchyard among the mountains are almost
all of them portraits. The clergyman and his family
described in Book VII. were among the poet's principal
associates in the vale of Grasmere. "There was much
talent in the family," says Wordsworth in the memoranda
dictated to Miss Fenwick; "and the eldest son was distinguished for poetical talent, of which a specimen is given
in my Notes to the *Sonnets on the Duddon*. Once when,
in our cottage at Townend, I was talking with him about
poetry, in the course of our conversation I presumed to
find fault with the versification of Pope, of whom he was
an enthusiastic admirer. He defended him with a warmth
that indicated much irritation; nevertheless I could not
abandon my point, and said, 'In compass and variety
of sound your own versification surpasses his.' Never
shall I forget the change in his countenance and tone of
voice. The storm was laid in a moment; he no longer
disputed my judgment; and I passed immediately in his
mind, no doubt, for as great a critic as ever lived."

It was with personages simple and unromantic as
these that Wordsworth filled the canvas of his longest
poem. Judged by ordinary standards the *Excursion*
appears an epic without action, and with two heroes,
the Pastor and the Wanderer, whose characters are
identical. Its form is cumbrous in the extreme, and
large tracts of it have little claim to the name of poetry.
Wordsworth compares the *Excursion* to a temple of which
his smaller poems form subsidiary shrines; but the reader
will more often liken the small poems to gems, and the
Excursion to the rock from which they were extracted.
The long poem contains, indeed, magnificent passages, but

as a whole it is a diffused description of scenery which
the poet has elsewhere caught in brighter glimpses ; a
diffused statement of hopes and beliefs which have crystallized more exquisitely elsewhere round moments of inspiring emotion. The *Excursion*, in short, has the draw-
backs of a didactic poem as compared with lyrical poems ;
but, judged as a didactic poem, it has the advantage of
containing teaching of true and permanent value.

I shall not attempt to deduce a settled scheme of philosophy from these discourses among the mountains. I
would urge only that as a guide to conduct Wordsworth's
precepts are not in themselves either unintelligible or
visionary. For whereas some moralists would have us
amend nature, and others bid us follow her, there is apt to
be something impracticable in the first maxim, and something vague in the second. Asceticism, quietism, enthusiasm, ecstasy—all systems which imply an unnatural
repression or an unnatural excitation of our faculties—are
ill-suited for the mass of mankind. And on the other
hand, if we are told to follow nature, to develope our
original character, we are too often in doubt as to which
of our conflicting instincts to follow, what part of our
complex nature to accept as our regulating self. But
Wordsworth, while impressing on us conformity to nature
as the rule of life, suggests a test of such conformity
which can be practically applied. " The child is father
of the man,"—in the words which stand as introduction
to his poetical works, and Wordsworth holds that the
instincts and pleasures of a healthy childhood sufficiently
indicate the lines on which our maturer character should be
formed. The joy which began in the mere sense of existence should be maintained by hopeful faith ; the simplicity
which began in inexperience should be recovered by medi-

tation ; the love which originated in the family circle
should expand itself over the race of men.   And the
calming and elevating influence of Nature—which to
Wordsworth's memory seemed the inseparable concomitant
of childish years—should be constantly invoked throughout life to keep the heart fresh and the eyes open to the
mysteries discernible through her radiant veil.   In a word,
the family affections, if duly fostered, the influences of
Nature, if duly sought, with some knowledge of the best
books, are material enough to "build up our moral being"
and to outweigh the less deep-seated impulses which prompt
to wrong-doing.

If, then, surrounding influences make so decisive a
difference in man's moral lot, what are we to say of those
who never have the chance of receiving those influences
aright ; who are reared, with little parental supervision, in
smoky cities, and spend their lives in confined and monotonous labour ?   One of the most impressive passages in
the *Excursion* is an indignant complaint of the injustice
thus done to the factory child.   Wordsworth was no
fanatical opponent of manufacturing industry.   He had
intimate friends among manufacturers ; and in one of his
letters he speaks of promising himself much pleasure from
witnessing the increased regard for the welfare of factory
hands of which one of these friends had set the example.
But he never lost sight of the fact that the life of the
mill-hand is an anomaly—is a life not in the order of
nature, and which requires to be justified by manifest
necessity and by continuous care.   The question to what
extent we may acquiesce in the continuance of a low order
of human beings, existing for our enjoyment rather than
for their own, may be answered with plausibility in very
different tones ; from the Communist who cannot acquiesce

in the inferiority of any one man's position to any other's, to the philosopher who holds that mankind has made the most eminent progress when a few chosen individuals have been supported in easy brilliancy by a population of serfs or slaves. Wordsworth's answer to this question is at once conservative and philanthropic. He holds to the distinction of classes, and thus admits a difference in the fulness and value of human lots. But he will not consent to any social arrangement which implies a necessary *moral* inferiority in any section of the body politic ; and he esteems it the statesman's first duty to provide that all citizens shall be placed under conditions of life which, however humble, shall not be unfavourable to virtue.

His views on national education, which at first sight appear so inconsistent, depend on the same conception of national welfare. Wordsworth was one of the earliest and most emphatic proclaimers of the duty of the State in this respect. The lines in which he insists that every child ought to be taught to read are, indeed, often quoted as an example of the moralizing baldness of much of his blank verse. But, on the other hand, when a great impulse was given to education (1820-30) by Bell and Lancaster, by the introduction of what was called the "Madras system" of tuition by pupil-teachers, and the spread of infant schools, Wordsworth was found unexpectedly in the opposite camp. Considering as he did all mental requirements as entirely subsidiary to moral progress, and in themselves of very little value, he objected to a system which, instead of confining itself to reading— that indispensable channel of moral nutriment—aimed at communicating knowledge as varied and advanced as time and funds would allow. He objected to the dissociation

of school and home life—to that relegation of domestic
interests and duties to the background, which large and
highly-organized schools, and teachers much above the
home level, must necessarily involve. And yet more
strongly, and, as it may still seem to many minds, with
convincing reason, he objected to an eleemosynary system,
which "precludes the poor mother from the strongest
motive human nature can be actuated by for industry, for
forethought, and self-denial." "The Spartan," he said,
" and other ancient communities, might disregard domestic
ties, because they had the substitution of country, which
we cannot have. Our course is to supplant domestic
attachments, without the possibility of substituting others
more capacious. What can grow out of it but selfishness? "
The half-century which has elapsed since Wordsworth
wrote these words has evidently altered the state of the
question. It has impressed on us the paramount necessity
of national education, for reasons political and social too
well known to repeat. But it may be feared that it has
also shifted the incidence of Wordsworth's arguments in a
more sinister manner, by vastly increasing the number of
those homes where domestic influence of the kind which
the poet saw around him at Rydal is altogether wanting
and school is the best avenue even to moral well-being.
" Heaven and hell," he writes in 1808, "are scarcely more
different from each other than Sheffield and Manchester,
&c., differ from the plains and valleys of Surrey, Essex,
Cumberland, or Westmoreland." It is to be feared, indeed, that even "the plains and valleys of Surrey and
Essex " contain many cottages whose spiritual and sanitary
conditions fall far short of the poet's ideal. But it is of
course in the great and growing centres of population that
the dangers which he dreads have come upon us in

their most aggravated form. And so long as there are in
England so many homes to which parental care and the
influences of Nature are alike unknown, no protest in
favour of the paramount importance of these primary
agencies in the formation of character can be regarded as
altogether out of date.

With such severe and almost prosaic themes is the
greater part of the *Excursion* occupied. Yet the poem is
far from being composed throughout in a prosaic spirit.
" Of its bones is coral made ;" its arguments and theories
have lain long in Wordsworth's mind, and have accreted
to themselves a rich investiture of observation and feeling.
Some of its passages rank among the poet's highest flights.
Such is the passage in Book I. describing the boy's rapture
at sunrise ; and the picture of a sunset at the close of the
same book.   Such is the opening of Book IV.; and the passage describing the wild joy of roaming through a mountain
storm ; and the metaphor in the same book which compares the mind's power of transfiguring the obstacles
which beset her, with the glory into which the moon
incorporates the umbrage that would intercept her
beams.

It would scarcely be possible at the present day that a
work containing such striking passages, and so much of
substance and elevation—however out of keeping it
might be with the ruling taste of the day—should appear
without receiving careful study from many quarters and
warm appreciation in some recognized organs of opinion.
Criticism in Wordsworth's day was both less competent
and less conscientious, and the famous " This will never
do " of Jeffrey in the *Edinburgh Review* was by no
means an extreme specimen of the general tone in which
the work was received.   The judgment of the reviewers

influenced popular taste ; and the book was as decided a
pecuniary failure as Wordsworth's previous ventures
had been.

And here, perhaps, is a fit occasion to speak of that
strangely violent detraction and abuse which formed so
large an ingredient in Wordsworth's life,—or rather, of
that which is the only element of permanent interest in
such a matter,—his manner of receiving and replying to
it. No writer, probably, who has afterwards achieved a
reputation at all like Wordsworth's, has been so long
represented by reviewers as purely ridiculous. And in
Wordsworth's manner of acceptance of this fact we may
discern all the strength, and something of the stiffness, of
his nature ; we may recognize an almost, but not quite,
ideal attitude under the shafts of unmerited obloquy.
For he who thus is arrogantly censured should remember
both the dignity and the frailty of man ; he should
wholly forgive, and almost wholly forget ; but, nevertheless,
should retain such serviceable hints as almost any criticism, however harsh or reckless, can afford, and go on his
way with no bitter broodings, but yet (to use Wordsworth's expression in another context) " with a melancholy in the soul, a sinking inward into ourselves from
thought to thought, a steady remonstrance, and a high
resolve."

How far his own self-assertion may becomingly be
carried in reply, is another and a delicate question. There
is almost necessarily something distasteful to us not only
in self-praise but even in a thorough self-appreciation.
We desire of the ideal character that his faculties of
admiration should be, as it were, absorbed in an eager
perception of the merits of others,—that a kind of shrink-
ing delicacy should prevent him from appraising his own

achievements with a similar care. Often, indeed, there is
something most winning in a touch of humorous blindness :
"Well, Miss Sophia, and how do *you* like the *Lady of
the Lake ?*"   "Oh, I've not read it; papa says there's
nothing so bad for young people as reading bad poetry."

But there are circumstances under which this graceful
absence of self-consciousness can no longer be maintained.
When a man believes that he has a message to deliver
that vitally concerns mankind, and when that message is
received with contempt and apathy, he is necessarily
driven back upon himself; he is forced to consider
whether what he has to say is after all so important, and
whether his mode of saying it be right and adequate. A
necessity of this kind was forced upon both Shelley and
Wordsworth. Shelley—the very type of self-forgetful
enthusiasm—was driven at last by the world's treatment
of him into a series of moods sometimes bitter and sometimes self-distrustful—into a sense of aloofness and detachment from the mass of men, which the poet who would
fain improve and exalt them should do his utmost not to
feel. On Wordsworth's more stubborn nature the effect
produced by many years of detraction was of a different
kind. Naturally introspective, he was driven by abuse
and ridicule into taking stock of himself more frequently
and more laboriously than ever. He formed an estimate
of himself and his writings which was, on the whole, (as
will now be generally admitted,) a just one ; and this view
he expressed when occasion offered—in sober language,
indeed, but with calm conviction, and with precisely the
same air of speaking from undoubted knowledge as when
he described the beauty of Cumbrian mountains or the
virtue of Cumbrian homes.

"It is impossible," he wrote to Lady Beaumont in 1807,

H

"that any expectations can be lower than mine concerning the immediate effect of this little work upon what is called the public. I do not here take into consideration the envy and malevolence, and all the bad passions which always stand in the way of a work of any merit from a living poet; but merely think of the pure, absolute, honest ignorance in which all worldlings, of every rank and situation, must be enveloped, with respect to the thoughts, feelings, and images on which the life of my poems depends. The things which I have taken, whether from within or without, what have they to do with routs, dinners, morning calls, hurry from door to door, from street to street, on foot or in carriage; with Mr. Pitt or Mr. Fox, Mr. Paul or Sir Francis Burdett, the Westminster election or the borough of Honiton? In a word —for I cannot stop to make my way through the hurry of images that present themselves to me—what have they to do with endless talking about things that nobody cares anything for, except as far as their own vanity is concerned, and this with persons they care nothing for, but as their vanity or *selfishness* is concerned? What have they to do (to say all at once) with a life without love? In such a life there can be no thought; for we have no thought (save thoughts of pain), but as far as we have love and admiration.

"It is an awful truth, that there neither is nor can be any genuine enjoyment of poetry among nineteen out of twenty of those persons who live, or wish to live, in the broad light of the world—among those who either are, or are striving to make themselves, people of consideration in society. This is a truth, and an awful one; because to be incapable of a feeling of poetry, in my sense of the word, is to be without love of human nature and reverence for God.

" Upon this I shall insist elsewhere ; at present let me confine myself to my object, which is to make you, my dear friend, as easy-hearted as myself with respect to these poems. Trouble not yourself upon their present reception. Of what moment is that compared with what I trust is their destiny ?—to console the afflicted ; to add sunshine to daylight, by making the happy happier ; to teach the young and the gracious of every age to see, to think, and feel, and, therefore, to become more actively and securely virtuous ; this is their office, which I trust they will faithfully perform, long after we (that is, all that is mortal of us,) are mouldered in our graves."

Such words as these come with dignity from the mouth of a man like Wordsworth when he has been, as it were, driven to bay,—when he is consoling an intimate friend, distressed at the torrent of ridicule which, as she fears, must sweep his self-confidence and his purposes away. He may be permitted to assure her that "my ears are stone-dead to this idle buzz, and my flesh as insensible as iron to these petty stings," and to accompany his assurance with a reasoned statement of the grounds of his unshaken hopes.

We feel, however, that such an expression of self-reliance on the part of a great man should be accompanied with some proof that no conceit or impatience is mixed with his steadfast calm. If he believes the public to be really unable to appreciate himself, he must show no surprise when they admire his inferiors ; he must remember that the case would be far worse if they admired no one at all. Nor must he descend from his own unpopular merits on the plea that after catching the public attention by what is bad he will retain it for what is good. If he is so sure that he is in the right he can afford to wait and let

the world come round to him. Wordsworth's conduct
satisfies both these tests. It is, indeed, curious to observe
how much abuse this inoffensive recluse received, and
how absolutely he avoided returning it. Byron, for
instance, must have seemed in his eyes guilty of something far more injurious to mankind than "a drowsy
frowsy poem, called the *Excursion*," could possibly appear.
But, except in one or two private letters, Wordsworth has
never alluded to Byron at all. Shelley's lampoon—a singular instance of the random blows of a noble spirit, striking at what, if better understood, it would eagerly have
revered—Wordsworth seems never to have read. Nor
did the violent attacks of the *Edinburgh* and the *Quarterly
Reviews* provoke him to any rejoinder. To " English Bards
and Scotch Reviewers"—leagued against him as their
common prey—he opposed a dignified silence; and the
only moral injury which he derived from their assaults lay
in that sense of the absence of trustworthy external
criticism which led him to treat everything which he had
once written down as if it were a special revelation, and to
insist with equal earnestness on his most trifling as on his
most important pieces—on *Goody Blake* and *The Idiot Boy*
as on *The Cuckoo* or *The Daffodils*. The sense of humour
is apt to be the first grace which is lost under persecution ;
and much of Wordsworth's heaviness and stiff exposition
of commonplaces is to be traced to a feeling, which he
could scarcely avoid, that "all day long he had lifted up
his voice to a perverse and gainsaying generation."

To the pecuniary loss inflicted on him by these adverse
criticisms he was justly sensible. He was far from
expecting, or even desiring, to be widely popular or to
make a rapid fortune ; but he felt that the labourer was
worthy of his hire, and that the devotion of years to

literature should have been met with some moderate
degree of the usual form of recognition which the world
accords to those who work for it. In 1820 he speaks of
"the whole of my returns from the writing trade not
amounting to seven-score pounds," and as late as 1843,
when at the height of his fame, he was not ashamed of
confessing the importance which he had always attached
to this particular.

"So sensible am I," he says, "of the deficiencies in all
that I write, and so far does everything that I attempt
fall short of what I wish it to be, that even private publication, if such a term may be allowed, requires more
resolution than I can command. I have written to give
vent to my own mind, and not without hope that, some
time or other, kindred minds might benefit by my
labours ; but I am inclined to believe I should never have
ventured to send forth any verses of mine to the world,
if it had not been done on the pressure of personal occasions. Had I been a rich man, my productions, like this
Epistle, the *Tragedy of the Borderers*, &c., would most
likely have been confined to manuscript."

An interesting passage from an unpublished letter of
Miss Wordsworth's, on the *White Doe of Rylstone*, confirms this statement :—

"My brother was very much pleased with your frankness in
telling us that you did not perfectly like his poem. He wishes
to know what your feelings were—whether the tale itself did
not interest you—or whether you could not enter into the conception of Emily's character, or take delight in that visionary
communion which is supposed to have existed between her and
the Doe. Do not fear to give him pain. He is far too much
accustomed to be abused to receive pain from it, (at least as far
as he himself is concerned.) My reason for asking you these
questions is, that some of our friends, who are equal admirers of

the *White Doe* and of my brother's published poems, think
that *this* poem will sell on account of the story; that is, that the
story will bear up those points which are above the level of the
public taste; whereas the two last volumes—except by a few
solitary individuals, who are passionately devoted to my
brother's works—are abused by wholesale.

"Now as his sole object in publishing this poem at present
would be for the sake of the money, he would not publish it if
he did not think, from the several judgments of his friends,
that it would be likely to have a sale. He has no pleasure in
publishing—he even detests it; and if it were not that he is *not*
over wealthy, he would leave all his works to be published after
his death. William himself is sure that the *White Doe* will
not sell or be admired, except by a very few, at first; and only
yields to Mary's entreaties and mine. We are determined, however, if we are deceived this time, to let him have his own way
in future."

These passages must be taken, no doubt, as representing
one aspect only of the poet's impulses in the matter.
With his deep conviction of the world's real, though un-
recognized, need of a pure vein of poetry, we can hardly
imagine him as permanently satisfied to defer his own contribution till after his death. Yet we may certainly
believe that the need of money helped him to overcome
much diffidence as to publication; and we may discern
something dignified in his frank avowal of this when it is
taken in connexion with his scrupulous abstinence from
any attempt to win the suffrages of the multitude by
means unworthy of his high vocation. He could never,
indeed, have written poems which could have vied in
immediate popularity with those of Byron or Scott. But
the criticisms on the first edition of the *Lyrical Ballads*
must have shown him that a slight alteration of method,—
nay even the excision of a few pages in each volume, pages
certain to be loudly objected to,—would have made a

marked difference in the sale and its proceeds. From this
point of view, even poems which we may now feel to
have been needlessly puerile and grotesque acquire a certain
impressiveness, when we recognize that the theory which
demanded their composition was one which their author
was willing to uphold at the cost of some years of real
physical privation, and of the postponement for a generation of his legitimate fame.

CHAPTER IX.

THE *Excursion* appeared in 1814, and in the course of
the next year Wordsworth republished his minor poems,
so arranged as to indicate the faculty of the mind which
he considered to have been predominant in the composition of each. To most readers this disposition has always
seemed somewhat arbitrary ; and it was once suggested to
Wordsworth that a chronological arrangement would be
better. The manner in which Wordsworth met this proposal indicated the limit of his absorption in himself—his
real desire only to dwell on his own feelings in such a
way as might make them useful to others. For he rejected the plan as too egotistical—as emphasizing the succession of moods in the poet's mind, rather than the
lessons which those moods could teach. His objection
points, at any rate, to a real danger which any man's
simplicity of character incurs by dwelling too attentively
on the changing phases of his own thought. But after
the writer's death the historical spirit will demand that
poems, like other artistic products, should be disposed for
the most part in the order of time.

In a Preface to this edition of 1815, and a Supplemen-
tary Essay, he developed the theory on poetry already set
forth in a well-known preface to the second edition of the

Lyrical Ballads. Much of the matter of these essays, received at the time with contemptuous aversion, is now accepted as truth; and few compositions of equal length con tain so much of vigorous criticism and sound reflection. It is only when they generalize too confidently that they are in danger of misleading us ; for all expositions of the art and practice of poetry must necessarily be incomplete. Poetry, like all the arts, is essentially a "mystery." Its charm depends upon qualities which we can neither define accurately nor reduce to rule nor create again at pleasure. Mankind, however, are unwilling to admit this ; and they endeavour from time to time to persuade themselves that they have discovered the rules which will enable them to produce the desired effect. And so much of the effect *can* thus be reproduced, that it is often possible to believe for a time that the problem has been solved. Pope, to take the instance which was prominent in Wordsworth's mind, was, by general admission, a poet. But his success seemed to depend on imitable peculiari· ties ; and Pope's imitators were so like Pope that it was hard to draw a line and say where they ceased to be poets. At last, however, this imitative school began to prove too much. If all the insipid verses which they wrote were poetry, what was the use of writing poetry at all ? A reaction succeeded, which asserted that poetry depends on emotion and not on polish ; that it consists precisely in those things which frigid imitators lack. Cowper, Burns, and Crabbe, (especially in his *Sir·Eustace Grey*), had preceded Wordsworth as leaders of this reaction. But they had acted half unconsciously, or had even at times themselves attempted to copy the very style which they were superseding.

Wordsworth, too, began with a tendency to imitate

Pope, but only in the school exercises which he wrote as a boy. Poetry soon became to him the expression of his own deep and simple feelings; and then he rebelled against rhetoric and unreality and found for himself a directer and truer voice. " I have proposed to myself to imitate and, as far as is possible, to adopt the very language of men. . . . I have taken as much pains to avoid what is usually called poetic diction as others ordinarily take to produce it." And he erected this practice into a general principle in the following passage :—

" I do not doubt that it may be safely affirmed that there neither is, nor can be, any essential difference between the language of prose and metrical composition. We are fond of tracing the resemblance between poetry and painting, and, accordingly, we call them sisters ; but where shall we find bonds of connexion sufficiently strict to typify the affinity between metrical and prose composition ? If it be affirmed that rhyme and metrical arrangement of themselves constitute a distinction which overturns what I have been saying on the strict affinity of metrical language with that of prose, and paves the way for other artificial distinctions which the mind voluntarily admits, I answer that the language of such poetry as I am recommending is, as far as is possible, a selection of the language really spoken by men ; that this selection, wherever it is made with true taste and feeling, will of itself form a distinction far greater than would at first be imagined, and will entirely separate the composition from the vulgarity and meanness of ordinary life; and if metre be superadded thereto, I believe that a dissimilitude will be produced altogether sufficient for the gratification of a rational mind. What other distinction would we have ? whence is it to come ? and where is it to exist ? "

There is a definiteness and simplicity about this description of poetry which may well make us wonder why this precious thing (producible, apparently, as easily as Pope's

imitators supposed, although by means different from
theirs) is not offered to us by more persons, and of better
quality. And it will not be hard to show that a good
poetical style must possess certain characteristics, which,
although something like them must exist in a good prose
style, are carried in poetry to a pitch so much higher as
virtually to need a specific faculty for their successful
production.

To illustrate the inadequacy of Wordsworth's theory to
explain the merits of his own poetry, I select a stanza
from one of his simplest and most characteristic poems—
The Affliction of Margaret :--

> Perhaps some dungeon hears thee groan,
> Maimed, mangled by inhuman men,
> Or thou upon a Desert thrown
> Inheritest the lion's Den ;
> Or hast been summoned to the Deep,
> Thou, thou and all thy mates, to keep
> An incommunicable sleep.

These lines, supposed to be uttered by "a poor widow
at Penrith," afford a fair illustration of what Wordsworth
calls "the language really spoken by men," with "metre
superadded." "What other distinction from prose," he
asks, "would we have ?" We may answer that we would
have what he has actually given us, viz., an appropriate
and attractive music, lying both in the rhythm and in the
actual sound of the words used,—a music whose complexity may be indicated here by drawing out some of its
elements in detail, at the risk of appearing pedantic and
technical. We observe, then (*a*), that the general movement of the lines is unusually slow. They contain a very
large proportion of strong accents and long vowels, to suit
the tone of deep and despairing sorrow. In six places

only out of twenty-eight is the accent weak where it
might be expected to be strong (in the second syllables,
namely, of the Iambic foot), and in each of these cases
the omission of a possible accent throws greater weight on
the next succeeding accent—on the accents, that is to say,
contained in the words inhuman, desert, lion, summoned,
deep, and sleep. (b) The first four lines contain subtle
alliterations of the letters d, h, m, and th. In this
connexion it should be remembered that when consonants
are thus repeated at the beginning of syllables, those
syllables need not be at the beginning of words; and
further, that repetitions scarcely more numerous than
chance alone would have occasioned, may be so placed by
the poet as to produce a strongly-felt effect. If any one
doubts the effectiveness of the unobvious alliterations
here insisted on, let him read (1) "jungle" for "desert,"
(2) "maybe" for "perhaps," (3) "tortured" for "man-
gled," (4) "blown" for "thrown," and he will become
sensible of the lack of the metrical support which the
existing consonants give one another. The three last lines
contain one or two similar alliterations on which I need not
dwell. (c) The words *inheritest* and *summoned* are by no
means such as "a poor widow," even at Penrith, would em-
ploy ; they are used to intensify the imagined relation which
connects the missing man with (1) the wild beasts who
surround him, and (2) the invisible Power which leads ; so
that something mysterious and awful is added to his fate.
(d) This impression is heightened by the use of the word
incommunicable in an unusual sense, "incapable of being
communicated *with*," instead of "incapable of being communicated ;" while (e) the expression "to keep an incommunicable sleep" for "to lie dead," gives dignity to the
occasion by carrying the mind back along a train of

literary associations of which the well-known ἀτέρμονα
νήγρετον ὕπνον of Moschus may be taken as the type.

We must not, of course, suppose that Wordsworth
consciously sought these alliterations, arranged these
accents, resolved to introduce an unusual word in the last
line, or hunted for a classical allusion. But what the
poet's brain does not do consciously it does unconsciously ;
a selective action is going on in its recesses simultaneously
with the overt train of thought, and on the degree of this
unconscious suggestiveness the richness and melody of the
poetry will depend.

No rules can secure the attainment of these effects; and
the very same artifices which are delightful when used by
one man seem mechanical and offensive when used by
another. Nor is it by any means always the case that
the man who can most delicately appreciate the melody of
the poetry of others will be able to produce similar melody
himself. Nay, even if he can produce it one year it by
no means follows that he will be able to produce it the
next. Of all qualifications for writing poetry this inven-
tive music is the most arbitrarily distributed, and the
most evanescent. But it is the more important to dwell
on its necessity, inasmuch as both good and bad poets are
tempted to ignore it. The good poet prefers to ascribe
his success to higher qualities ; to his imagination, elevation of thought, descriptive faculty. The bad poet can
more easily urge that his thoughts are too advanced for
mankind to appreciate than that his melody is too sweet
for their ears to catch. And when the gift vanishes no
poet is willing to confess that it is gone; so humiliating
is it to lose power over mankind by the loss of something
which seems quite independent of intellect or character.
And yet so it is. For some twenty years at most (1798-

1818), Wordsworth possessed this gift of melody. During those years he wrote works which profoundly influenced mankind. The gift then left him ; he continued as wise and as earnest as ever, but his poems had no longer any potency, nor his existence much public importance.

Humiliating as such reflections may seem, they are in accordance with actual experience in all branches of art. The fact is that the pleasures which art gives us are complex in the extreme. We are always disposed to dwell on such of their elements as are explicable and can in some way be traced to moral or intellectual sources. But they contain also other elements which are inexplicable, non-moral, and non-intellectual, and which render most of our attempted explanations of artistic merit so incomplete as to be practically misleading. Among such incomplete explanations Wordsworth's essays must certainly be ranked. It would not be safe for any man to believe that he had produced true poetry because he had fulfilled the conditions which Wordsworth lays down. But the essays effected what is perhaps as much as the writer on art can fairly hope to accomplish. They placed in a striking light that side of the subject which had been too long ignored ; they aided in recalling an art which had become conventional and fantastic into the normal current of English thought and speech.

It may be added that both in doctrine and practice Wordsworth exhibits a progressive reaction from the extreme views with which he starts towards that common vein of good sense and sound judgment which may be traced back to Horace, Longinus, and Aristotle. His first preface is violently polemic. He attacks with reason that conception of the sublime and beautiful which is represented by Dryden's picture of " Cortes alone in his night-

gown," remarking that " the mountains seem to nod their
drowsy heads." But the only example of true poetry
which he sees fit to adduce in contrast consists in a stanza
from the *Babes in the Wood.* In his preface of 1815 he
is not less severe on false sentiment and false observation.
But his views of the complexity and dignity of poetry
have been much developed, and he is willing now to draw
his favourable instances from Shakespeare, Milton, Virgil,
and himself.

His own practice underwent a corresponding change.
It is only to a few poems of his earlier years that the
famous parody of the *Rejected Addresses* fairly applies.

> My father's walls are made of brick,
> But not so tall and not so thick
> As these ; and goodness me !
> My father's beams are made of wood,
> But never, never half so good
> As those that now I see !

Lines something like these might have occurred in *The
Thorn* or *The Idiot Boy.* Nothing could be more different
from the style of the sonnets, or of the *Ode to Duty*, or
of *Laodamia.* And yet both the simplicity of the earlier
and the pomp of the later poems were almost always
noble ; nor is the transition from the one style to the
other a perplexing or abnormal thing. For all sincere
styles are congruous to one another, whether they be
adorned or no, as all high natures are congruous to one
another, whether in the garb of peasant or of prince.
What is incongruous to both is affectation, vulgarity,
egoism ; and while the noble style can be interchangeably
childlike or magnificent, as its theme requires, the ignoble
can neither simplify itself into purity nor deck itself into
grandeur.

It need not, therefore, surprise us to find the classical
models becoming more and more dominant in Wordsworth's mind, till the poet of *Poor Susan* and *The Cuckoo*
spends months over the attempt to translate the *Æneid,*—
to win the secret of that style which he placed at the head
of all poetic styles, and of those verses which " wind," as
he says, "with the majesty of the Conscript Fathers
entering the Senate-house in solemn procession," and
envelope in their imperial melancholy all the sorrows and
the fates of man.

And, indeed, so tranquil and uniform was the life which
we are now retracing, and at the same time so receptive
of any noble influence which opportunity might bring,
that a real epoch is marked in Wordsworth's poetical career
by the mere re-reading of some Latin authors in 1814-16
with a view to preparing his eldest son for the University.   Among the poets whom he thus studied was one in
whom he might seem to discern his own spirit endowed
with grander proportions, and meditating on sadder fates.
Among the poets of the battlefield, of the study, of the
boudoir, he encountered the first Priest of Nature, the
first poet in Europe who had deliberately shunned the
life of courts and cities for the mere joy in Nature's
presence, for "sweet Parthenope and the fields beside
Vesevus' hill."

There are, indeed, passages in the *Georgics* so Wordsworthian, as we now call it, in tone, that it is hard to
realize what centuries separated them from the *Sonnet to
Lady Beaumont* or from *Ruth*.   Such, for instance, is the
picture of the Corycian old man, who had made himself
independent of the seasons by his gardening skill, so that
" when gloomy winter was still rending the stones with
frost, still curbing with ice the rivers' onward flow, he

even then was plucking the soft hyacinth's bloom, and
chid the tardy summer and delaying airs of spring." Such,
again, is the passage where the poet breaks from the glories
of successful industry into the delight of watching the
great processes which nature accomplishes untutored and
alone, " the joy of gazing on Cytorus waving with boxwood,
and on forests of Narycian pine, on tracts that never felt
the harrow, nor knew the care of man."

Such thoughts as these the Roman and the English
poet had in common ;—the heritage of untarnished souls.

> I asked ; 'twas whispered ; The device
> To each and all might well belong :
> It is the Spirit of Paradise
> That prompts such work, a Spirit strong,
> That gives to all the self-same bent
> Where life is wise and innocent.

It is not only in tenderness but in dignity that the
" wise and innocent" are wont to be at one. Strong in
tranquillity, they can intervene amid great emotions with
a master's voice, and project on the storm of passion the
clear light of their unchanging calm. And thus it was
that the study of Virgil, and especially of Virgil's solemn
picture of the Underworld, prompted in Wordsworth's
mind the most majestic of his poems, his one great utter-
ance on heroic love.

He had as yet written little on any such topic as this.
At Goslar he had composed the poems on *Lucy* to
which allusion has already been made. And after his
happy marriage he had painted in one of the best known
of his poems the sweet transitions of wedded love, as it
moves on from the first shock and agitation of the encounter of predestined souls through all tendernesses of
intimate affection into a pervading permanency and calm.

I

Scattered, moreover, throughout his poems are several passages in which the passion is treated with similar force and truth. The poem which begins " 'Tis said that some have died for love " depicts the enduring poignancy of bereavement with an " iron pathos " that is almost too strong for art. And something of the same power of clinging attachment is shown in the sonnet where the poet is stung with the thought that " even for the least division of an hour" he has taken pleasure in the life around him, without the accustomed tacit reference to one who has passed away. There is a brighter touch of constancy in that other sonnet where, after letting his fancy play over a glad imaginary past, he turns to his wife, ashamed that even in so vague a vision he could have shaped for himself a solitary joy.

> Let *her* be comprehended in the frame
> Of these illusions, or they please no more.

In later years the two sonnets on his wife's picture set on that love the consecration of faithful age ; and there are those who can recall his look as he gazed on the picture and tried to recognize in that aged face the Beloved who to him was ever young and fair,—a look as of one dwelling in life-long affections with the unquestioning single-heartedness of a child.

And here it might have been thought that as his experience ended his power of description would have ended too. But it was not so. Under the powerful stimulus of the sixth *Æneid*—allusions to which pervade *Laodamia* [2]

---

[2] *Laodamia* should be read (as it is given in Mr. Matthew Arnold's admirable volume of selections) with the *earlier* conclusion : the *second* form is less satisfactory, and the *third*, with its sermonizing tone, " thus all in vain exhorted and reproved," is worst of all.

throughout—with unusual labour, and by a strenuous
effort of the imagination, Wordsworth was enabled to
depict his own love *in excelsis*, to imagine what aspect
it might have worn, if it had been its destiny to deny
itself at some heroic call, and to confront with nobleness
an extreme emergency, and to be victor (as Plato has it)
in an Olympian contest of the soul. For, indeed, the
" fervent, not ungovernable, love," which is the ideal that
Protesilaus is sent to teach, is on a great scale the same
affection which we have been considering in domesticity
and peace ; it is love considered not as a revolution but
as a consummation ; as a self-abandonment not to a laxer
but to a sterner law ; no longer as an invasive passion, but
as the deliberate habit of the soul.   It is that conception
of love which springs into being in the last canto of
Dante's *Purgatory*,—which finds in English chivalry a
noble voice,—

> I could not love thee, dear, so much,
> Loved I not honour more.

For, indeed, (even as Plato says that Beauty is the splendour of Truth,) so such a Love as this is the splendour of
Virtue ; it is the unexpected spark that flashes from self-
forgetful soul to soul, it is man's standing evidence that
he "must lose himself to find himself," and that only
when the veil of his personality has lifted from around
him can he recognize that he is already in heaven.

In a second poem inspired by this revived study of
classical antiquity Wordsworth has traced the career of
Dion,—the worthy pupil of Plato, the philosophic ruler of
Syracuse, who allowed himself to shed blood unjustly,
though for the public good, and was haunted by a spectre
symbolical of this fatal error.   At last Dion was assassi-

nated, and the words in which the poet tells his fate seem
to me to breathe the very triumph of philosophy, to paint
with a touch the greatness of a spirit which makes of
Death himself a deliverer, and has its strength in the
unseen.

> So were the hopeless troubles, that involved
> The soul of Dion, instantly dissolved.

I can only compare these lines to that famous passage
of Sophocles where the lamentations of the dying Œdipus
are interrupted by the impatient summons of an unseen
accompanying god.   In both places the effect is the same ;
to present to us with striking brevity the contrast between
the visible and the invisible presences that may stand
about a man's last hour ; for he may feel with the desolate Œdipus that " all I am has perished "—he may sink
like Dion through inextricable sadness to a disastrous
death, and then in a moment the transitory shall disappear
and the essential shall be made plain, and from Dion's
upright spirit the perplexities shall vanish away, and
Œdipus, in the welcome of that unknown companionship,
shall find his expiations over and his reward begun.

It is true, no doubt, that when Wordsworth wrote these
poems he had lost something of the young inimitable
charm which fills such pieces as the *Fountain* or the
Solitary Reaper.   His language is majestic, but it is no
longer magical.   And yet we cannot but feel that he has
put into these poems something which he could not have
put into the poems which preceded them; that they bear
the impress of a soul which has added moral effort to
poetic inspiration, and is mistress now of the acquired as
well as of the innate virtue.   For it is words like these
that are the strength and stay of men; nor can their

accent of lofty earnestness be simulated by the writer's art.
Literary skill may deceive the reader who seeks a literary
pleasure alone ; and he to whom these strong consolations
are a mere imaginative luxury may be uncertain or indifferent out of what heart they come. But those who
need them know ; spirits that hunger after righteousness
discern their proper food; there is no fear lest they con-
found the sentimental and superficial with those weighty
utterances of moral truth which are the most precious
legacy that a man can leave to mankind.

Thus far, then, I must hold that although much of
grace had already vanished there was on the whole a
progress and elevation in the mind of him of whom we
treat. But the culminating point is here. After this—
whatever ripening process may have been at work unseen—
what is chiefly visible is the slow stiffening of the imaginative power, the slow withdrawal of the insight into
the soul of things, and a descent—ἀβληχρὸς μάλα τοῖος—
" soft as soft can be," to the euthanasy of a death that
was like sleep.

The impression produced by Wordsworth's reperusal of
Virgil in 1814-16 was a deep and lasting one. In
1829-30 he devoted much time and labour to a translation of the first three books of the *Æneid*, and it is
interesting to note the gradual modification of his views
as to the true method of rendering poetry.

" I have long been persuaded," he writes to Lord Lonsdale in 1829, " that Milton formed his blank verse upon
the model of the *Georgics* and the *Æneid*, and I am so
much struck with this resemblance, that I should have
attempted Virgil in blank verse, had I not been persuaded
that no ancient author can with advantage be so rendered.
Their religion, their warfare, their course of action and

feeling, are too remote from modern interest to allow it. We require every possible help and attraction of sound in our language to smooth the way for the admission of things so remote from our present concerns. My own notion of translation is, that it cannot be too literal, provided these faults be avoided : *baldness*, in which I include all that takes from dignity ; and strangeness, or uncouthness, including harshness ; and lastly, attempts to convey meanings which, as they cannot be given but by languid circumlocutions, cannot in fact be said to be given at all. . . . I feel it, however, to be too probable that my translation is deficient in ornament, because I must unavoidably have lost many of Virgil's, and have never without reluctance attempted a compensation of my own."

The truth of this last self-criticism is very apparent from the fragments of the translation which were published in the *Philological Museum ;* and Coleridge, to whom the whole manuscript was submitted, justly complains of finding "page after page without a single brilliant note ;" and adds, "Finally, my conviction is that you undertake an impossibility, and that there is no medium between a pure version and one on the avowed principle of *compensation* in the widest sense, i. e. manner, genius, total effect ; I confine myself to *Virgil* when I say this." And it appears that Wordsworth himself came round to this view, for in reluctantly sending a specimen of his work to the *Philological Museum* in 1832, he says,—

"Having been displeased in modern translations with the additions of incongruous matter, I began to translate with a resolve to keep clear of that fault by adding nothing ; but I became convinced that a spirited translation can scarcely be accomplished in the English language without admitting a principle of compensation."

There is a curious analogy between the experiences of
Cowper and Wordsworth in the way of translation.
Wordsworth's translation of Virgil was prompted by the
same kind of reaction against the reckless laxity of Dryden
as that which inspired Cowper against the distorting
artificiality of Pope. In each case the new translator
cared more for his author and took a much higher view
of a translator's duty than his predecessor had done. But
in each case the plain and accurate translation was a
failure, while the loose and ornate one continued to be
admired. We need not conclude from this that the wilful
inaccuracy of Pope or Dryden would be any longer ex-
cusable in such a work. But on the other hand we may
certainly feel that nothing is gained by rendering an ancient
poet into verse at all unless that verse be of a quality to
give a pleasure independent of the faithfulness of the
translation which it conveys.

The translations and *Laodamia* are not the only indications of the influence which Virgil exercised over Wordsworth. Whether from mere similarity of feeling, or from
more or less conscious recollection, there are frequent
passages in the English which recall the Roman poet.
Who can hear Wordsworth describe how a poet on the
island in Grasmere

> At noon
> Spreads out his limbs, while, yet unshorn, the sheep,
> Panting beneath the burthen of their wool
> Lie round him, even as if they were a part
> Of his own household :—

and not think of the stately tenderness of Virgil's

> Stant et oves circum ; nostri nec pœnitet illas—

and the flocks of Arcady that gather round in sympathy
with the lovelorn Gallus' woe ?

So again the well-known lines—

> Not seldom, clad in radiant vest,
> Deceitfully goes forth the Morn;
> Not seldom Evening in the west
> Sinks smilingly forsworn,—

are almost a translation of Palinurus' remonstrance with
"the treachery of tranquil heaven." And when the poet
wishes for any link which could bind him closer to the
Highland maiden who has flitted across his path as a being
of a different world from his own :—

> Thine elder Brother would I be,
> Thy Father, anything to thee!—

we hear the echo of the sadder plaint—

> Atque utinam e vobis unus—

when the Roman statesman longs to be made one with the
simple life of shepherd or husbandman, and to know
their undistracted joy.

Still more impressive is the shock of surprise with
which we read in Wordsworth's poem on Ossian the
following lines :—

> Musæus, stationed with his lyre
> Supreme among the Elysian quire,
> Is, for the dwellers upon earth,
> Mute as a lark ere morning's birth,

and perceive that he who wrote them has entered—where
no commentator could conduct him—into the solemn
pathos of Virgil's *Musæum ante omnis*— ; where the
singer whose very existence upon earth has become a
legend and a mythic name is seen keeping in the underworld his old pre-eminence, and towering above the blessed
dead.

This is a stage in Wordsworth's career on which his biographer is tempted unduly to linger. For we have reached the Indian summer of his genius; it can still shine at moments bright as ever, and with even a new majesty and calm; but we feel, nevertheless, that the melody is dying from his song; that he is hardening into self-repetition, into rhetoric, into sermonizing common-place, and is rigid where he was once profound. The *Thanksgiving Ode* (1816) strikes death to the heart. The accustomed patriotic sentiments—the accustomed virtuous aspirations—these are still there; but the accent is like that of a ghost who calls to us in hollow mimicry of a voice that once we loved.

And yet Wordsworth's poetic life was not to close without a great symbolical spectacle, a solemn farewell. Sunset among the Cumbrian hills, often of remarkable beauty, once or twice, perhaps, in a score of years, reaches a pitch of illusion and magnificence which indeed seems nothing less than the commingling of earth and heaven. Such a sight—seen from Rydal Mount in 1818—afforded once more the needed stimulus, and evoked that "*Evening Ode, composed on an evening of extraordinary splendour and beauty*," which is the last considerable production of Wordsworth's genius. In this ode we recognize the peculiar gift of reproducing with magical simplicity as it were the inmost virtue of natural phenomena.

> No sound is uttered, but a deep
> And solemn harmony pervades
> The hollow vale from steep to steep,
> And penetrates the glades.
> Far distant images draw nigh,
> Called forth by wondrous potency
> Of beamy radiance, that imbues
> Whate'er it strikes, with gem-like hues!

In vision exquisitely clear
Herds range along the mountain side ;
And glistening antlers are descried,
And gilded flocks appear.

Once more the poet brings home to us that sense of
belonging at once to two worlds, which gives to human
life so much of mysterious solemnity.

Wings at my shoulder seem to play ;
But, rooted here, I stand and gaze
On those bright steps that heavenward raise
Their practicable way.

And the poem ends—with a deep personal pathos—in an
allusion, repeated from the *Ode on Immortality*, to the
light which "lay about him in his infancy,"—the light

Full early lost, and fruitlessly deplored ;
Which at this moment, on my waking sight
Appears to shine, by miracle restored !
My soul, though yet confined to earth,
Rejoices in a second birth ;
—'Tis past, the visionary splendour fades ;
And night approaches with her shades.

For those to whom the mission of Wordsworth appears
before all things as a religious one there is something
solemn in the spectacle of the seer standing at the close of
his own apocalypse, with the consciousness that the
stiffening brain would never permit him to drink again
that overflowing sense of glory and revelation ; never, till
he should drink it new in the kingdom of God.   He lived,
in fact, through another generation of men, but the vision
came to him no more.

Or if some vestige of those gleams
Survived, 'twas only in his dreams.

We look on a man's life for the most part as forming in itself a completed drama. We love to see the interest maintained to the close, the pathos deepened at the departing hour. To die on the same day is the prayer of lovers, to vanish at Trafalgar is the ideal of heroic souls. And yet—so wide and various are the issues of life—there is a solemnity as profound in a quite different lot. For if we are moving among eternal emotions we should have time to bear witness that they are eternal. Even Love left desolate may feel with a proud triumph that it could never have rooted itself so immutably amid the joys of a visible return as it can do through the constancies of bereavement, and the lifelong memory which is a lifelong hope. And Vision, Revelation, Ecstasy,—it is not only while these are kindling our way that we should speak of them to men, but rather when they have passed from us and left us only their record in our souls, whose permanence confirms the fiery finger which wrote it long ago. For as the Greeks would end the first drama of a trilogy with a hush of concentration, and with declining notes of calm, so to us the narrowing receptivity and persistent steadfastness of age suggest not only decay but expectancy, and not death so much as sleep; or seem, as it were, the beginning of operations which are not measured by our hurrying time, nor tested by any achievement to be accomplished here.

CHAPTER X.

IT will have been obvious from the preceding pages, as well as from the tone of other criticisms on Wordsworth, that his exponents are not content to treat his poems on Nature simply as graceful descriptive pieces, but speak of him in terms usually reserved for the originators of some great religious movement. " The very image of Wordsworth," says De Quincey, for instance, " as I prefigured it to my own planet-struck eye, crushed my faculties as before Elijah or St. Paul." How was it that poems so simple in outward form that the reviewers of the day classed them with the *Song of Sixpence*, or at best with the *Babes in the Wood*, could affect a critic like De Quincey,—I do not say with admiration, but with this exceptional sense of revelation and awe ?

The explanation of this anomaly lies, as is well known, in something new and individual in the way in which Wordsworth regarded Nature ; something more or less discernible in most of his works, and redeeming even some of the slightest of them from insignificance, while conferring on the more serious and sustained pieces an importance of a different order from that which attaches to even the most brilliant productions of his contemporaries. To define with exactness, however, what was this new

element imported by our poet into man's view of Nature
is far from easy, and requires some brief consideration of
the attitude in this respect of his predecessors.

There is so much in the external world which is terrible
or unfriendly to man, that the first impression made on
him by Nature as a whole, even in temperate climates, is
usually that of awfulness; his admiration being reserved
for the fragments of her which he has utilized for his
own purposes, or adorned with his own handiwork.
When Homer tells us of a place

> Where even a god might gaze, and stand apart,
> And feel a wondering rapture at the heart,

it is of no prospect of sea or mountain that he is speaking, but of a garden where everything is planted in rows,
and there is a never-ending succession of pears and figs.
These gentler aspects of Nature will have their minor
deities to represent them; but the men, of whatever race
they be, whose minds are most absorbed in the problems
of man's position and destiny will tend for the most part
to some sterner and more overwhelming conception of the
sum of things. "Lord, what is man that Thou art mindful
of him?" is the cry of Hebrew piety as well as of modern
science; and the "majestas cognita rerum,"—the recognized majesty of the universe—teaches Lucretius only
the indifference of gods and the misery of men.

But in a well-known passage, in which Lucretius is
honoured as he deserves, we find nevertheless a different
view hinted, with an impressiveness which it had hardly
acquired till then. We find Virgil implying that scientific knowledge of Nature may not be the only way of
arriving at the truth about her; that her loveliness is also
a revelation, and that the soul which is in unison with

her is justified by its own peace. This is the very substance of *The Poet's Epitaph* also ; of the poem in which Wordsworth at the beginning of his career describes himself as he continued till its close,—the poet who " murmurs near the running brooks a music sweeter than their own,"—who scorns the man of science " who would peep and botanize upon his mother's grave."

> The outward shows of sky and earth,
> Of hill and valley, he has viewed ;
> And impulses of deeper birth
> Have come to him in solitude.
>
> In common things that round us lie
> Some random truths he can impart,—
> The harvest of a quiet eye
> That broods and sleeps on his own heart.
>
> But he is weak, both man and boy,
> Hath been an idler in the land ;
> Contented if he might enjoy
> The things which others understand.

Like much else in the literature of imperial Rome, the passage in the second *Georgic* to which I have referred is in its essence more modern than the Middle Ages. Mediæval Christianity involved a divorce from the nature around us, as well as from the nature within. With the rise of the modern spirit delight in the external world returns ; and from Chaucer downwards through the whole course of English poetry are scattered indications of a mood which draws from visible things an intuition of things not seen. When Withers, in words which Wordsworth has fondly quoted, says of his muse,—

> By the murmur of a spring,
> Or the least bough's rustelling ;

> By a daisy whose leaves spread,
> Shut when Titan goes to bed;
> Or a shady bush or tree,—
> She could more infuse in me
> Than all Nature's beauties can
> In some other wiser man,—

he felt already, as Wordsworth after him, that Nature is
no mere collection of phenomena, but infuses into her
least approaches some sense of her mysterious whole.

Passages like this, however, must not be too closely
pressed. The mystic element in English literature has
run for the most part into other channels; and when,
after Pope's reign of artificiality and convention, attention
was redirected to the phenomena of Nature by Collins,
Beattie, Thomson, Crabbe, Cowper, Burns, and Scott, it
was in a spirit of admiring observation rather than of an
intimate worship. Sometimes, as for the most part in
Thomson, we have mere picturesqueness,—a reproduction
of Nature for the mere pleasure of reproducing her,—a
kind of stock-taking of her habitual effects. Or sometimes, as in Burns, we have a glowing spirit which looks
on Nature with a side glance, and uses her as an accessory
to the expression of human love and woe. Cowper
sometimes contemplated her as a whole, but only as
affording a proof of the wisdom and goodness of a personal Creator.

To express what is characteristic in Wordsworth we
must recur to a more generalized conception of the relations between the natural and the spiritual worlds. We
must say with Plato—the lawgiver of all subsequent
idealists—that the unknown realities around us, which
the philosopher apprehends by the contemplation of
abstract truth, become in various ways obscurely perceptible to men under the influence of " divine mad-

ness,"—of an enthusiasm which is in fact inspiration.
And further, giving, as he so often does, a half-fanciful
expression to a substance of deep meaning,—Plato dis-
tinguishes four kinds of this enthusiasm. There is the
prophet's glow of revelation; and the prevailing prayer
which averts the wrath of heaven; and that philosophy
which enters, so to say, unawares into the poet through
his art, and into the lover through his love. Each of
these stimuli may so exalt the inward faculties as to make
a man ἔνθεος καὶ ἔκφρων,—"bereft of reason but filled
with divinity,"—percipient of an intelligence other and
larger than his own. To this list Wordsworth has
made an important addition. He has shown by his
example and writings that the contemplation of Nature
may become a stimulus as inspiring as these; may enable
us "to see into the life of things"—as far, perhaps, as
beatific vision or prophetic rapture can attain. Assertions
so impalpable as these must justify themselves by sub-
jective evidence. He who claims to give a message must
satisfy us that he has himself received it; and, inasmuch
as transcendent things are in themselves inexpressible,
he must convey to us in hints and figures the conviction
which we need. Prayer may bring the spiritual world
near to us; but when the eyes of the kneeling Dominic
seem to say "*Io son venuto a questo*," their look must
persuade us that the life of worship has indeed attained
the reward of vision. Art, too, may be inspired; but
the artist, in whatever field he works, must have "such a
mastery of his mystery" that the fabric of his imagination
stands visible in its own light before our eyes,—

> Seeing it is built
> Of music; therefore never built at all,
> And, therefore, built for ever.

Love may open heaven; but when the lover would invite
us "thither, where are the eyes of Beatrice," he must
make us feel that his individual passion is indeed part
and parcel of that love "which moves the sun and the
other stars."

And so also with Wordsworth. Unless the words
which describe the intense and sympathetic gaze with
which he contemplates Nature convince us of the reality
of "the light which never was on sea or land,"—of the
"Presence which disturbs him with the joy of elevated
thoughts,"—of the authentic vision of those hours

> When the light of sense
> Goes out, but with a flash that has revealed
> The invisible world ;—

unless his tone awakes a responsive conviction in ourselves, there is no argument by which he can prove to us
that he is offering a new insight to mankind. Yet, on
the other hand, it need not be unreasonable to see in his
message something more than a mere individual fancy.
It seems, at least, to be closely correlated with those other
messages of which we have spoken,—those other cases
where some original element of our nature is capable of
being regarded as an inlet of mystic truth. For in each
of these complex aspects of religion we see, perhaps, the
modification of a primeval instinct. There is a point
of view from which Revelation seems to be but transfigured Sorcery, and Love transfigured Appetite, and
Philosophy man's ordered Wonder, and Prayer his
softening Fear. And similarly in the natural religion
of Wordsworth we may discern the modified outcome
of other human impulses hardly less universal—of those
instincts which led our forefathers to people earth and air

with deities, or to vivify the whole universe with a single
soul. In this view the achievement of Wordsworth was
of a kind which most of the moral leaders of the race
have in some way or other performed. It was that he
turned a theology back again into a religion; that he revived in a higher and purer form those primitive elements
of reverence for Nature's powers which had diffused themselves into speculation, or crystallized into mythology;
that for a system of beliefs about Nature, which paganism
had allowed to become grotesque,—of rites which had
become unmeaning,—he substituted an admiration for
Nature so constant, an understanding of her so subtle, a
sympathy so profound, that they became a veritable worship. Such worship, I repeat, is not what we commonly
imply either by paganism or by pantheism. For in pagan
countries, though the gods may have originally represented natural forces, yet the conception of them soon
becomes anthropomorphic, and they are reverenced as
transcendent *men;* and, on the other hand, pantheism is
generally characterized by an indifference to things in the
concrete, to Nature in detail; so that the Whole, or Universe, with which the Stoics (for instance) sought to be
in harmony, was approached not by contemplating external objects, but rather by ignoring them.

Yet here I would be understood to speak only in the
most general manner. So congruous in all ages are the
aspirations and the hopes of men that it would be
rash indeed to attempt to assign the moment when
any spiritual truth rises for the first time on human
consciousness. But thus much, I think, may be fairly
said, that the maxims of Wordsworth's form of natural
religion were uttered before Wordsworth only in the sense
in which the maxims of Christianity were uttered before

Christ. To compare small things with great—or rather, to compare great things with things vastly greater—the essential spirit of the *Lines near Tintern Abbey* was for practical purposes as new to mankind as the essential spirit of the *Sermon on the Mount*. Not the isolated expression of moral ideas, but their fusion into a whole in one memorable personality, is that which connects them for ever with a single name. Therefore it is that Wordsworth is venerated; because to so many men—indifferent, it may be, to literary or poetical effects, as such—he has shown by the subtle intensity of his own emotion how the contemplation of Nature can be made a revealing agency, like Love or Prayer,—an opening, if indeed there be any opening, into the transcendent world.

The prophet with such a message as this will, of course, appeal for the most part to the experience of exceptional moments—those moments when "we see into the life of things;" when the face of Nature sends to us "gleams like the flashing of a shield;"—hours such as those of the Solitary, who, gazing on the lovely distant scene,

> Would gaze till it became
> Far lovelier, and his heart could not sustain
> The beauty, still more beauteous.

But the idealist, of whatever school, is seldom content to base his appeal to us upon these scattered intuitions alone. There is a whole epoch of our existence whose memories, differing, indeed, immensely in vividness and importance in the minds of different men, are yet sufficiently common to all men to form a favourite basis for philosophical argument. "The child is father of the man;" and through the recollection and observation of early childhood we may hope to trace our ancestry—in

heaven above or on the earth beneath—in its most significant manifestation.

It is to the workings of the mind of the child that the
philosopher appeals who wishes to prove that knowledge
is recollection, and that our recognition of geometrical
truths—so prompt as to appear instinctive—depends on
our having been actually familiar with them in an earlier
world. The Christian mystic invokes with equal confidence his own memories of a state which seemed as yet
to know no sin :—

> Happy those early days, when I
> Shined in my angel infancy !
> Before I understood this place
> Appointed for my second race,
> Or taught my soul to fancy aught
> But a white, celestial thought ;
> When yet I had not walked above
> A mile or two from my first Love,
> And looking back at that short space
> Could see a glimpse of His bright face ;
> When on some gilded cloud or flower
> My gazing soul would dwell an hour,
> And in those weaker glories spy
> Some shadows of eternity ;
> Before I taught my tongue to wound
> My conscience with a sinful sound,
> Or had the black art to dispense
> A several sin to every sense,
> But felt through all this fleshly dress
> Bright shoots of everlastingness.

And Wordsworth, whose recollections were exceptionally vivid, and whose introspection was exceptionally
penetrating, has drawn from his own childish memories
philosophical lessons which are hard to disentangle in a
logical statement, but which will roughly admit of being
classed under two heads. For, firstly, he has shown an

unusual delicacy of analysis in eliciting the "firstborn affinities that fit our new existence to existing things ;"— in tracing the first impact of impressions which are destined to give the mind its earliest ply, or even, in unreflecting natures, to determine the permanent modes of thought. And, secondly, from the halo of pure and vivid emotions with which our childish years are surrounded, and the close connexion of this emotion with external nature, which it glorifies and transforms, he infers that the soul has enjoyed elsewhere an existence superior to that of earth, but an existence of which external nature retains for a time the power of reminding her.

The first of these lines of thought may be illustrated by a passage in the *Prelude*, in which the boy's mind is represented as passing through precisely the train of emotion which we may imagine to be at the root of the theology of many barbarous peoples. He is rowing at night alone on Esthwaite Lake, his eyes fixed upon a ridge of crags, above which nothing is visible :—

> I dipped my oars into the silent lake,
> And as I rose upon the stroke my boat
> Went heaving through the water like a swan ;—
> When, from behind that craggy steep till then
> The horizon's bound, a huge peak, black and huge,
> As if with voluntary power instinct
> Upreared its head. I struck and struck again ;
> And, growing still in stature, the grim shape
> Towered up between me and the stars, and still,
> For so it seemed, with purpose of its own,
> And measured motion like a living thing,
> Strode after me. With trembling oars I turned,
> And through the silent water stole my way
> Back to the covert of the willow-tree ;
> There in her mooring-place I left my bark,
> And through the meadows homeward went, in grave
> And serious mood. But after I had seen

That spectacle, for many days, my brain
Worked with a dim and undetermined sense
Of unknown modes of being ; o'er my thoughts
There hung a darkness—call it solitude,
Or blank desertion. No familiar shapes
Remained, no pleasant images of trees,
Of sea, or sky, no colours of green fields ;
Put huge and mighty forms, that do not live
Like living men, moved slowly thro' the mind
By day, and were a trouble to my dreams.

In the controversy as to the origin of the worship of
inanimate objects, or of the powers of Nature, this passage
might fairly be cited as an example of the manner in
which those objects, or those powers, can impress the
mind with that awe which is the foundation of savage
creeds, while yet they are not identified with any human
intelligence, such as the spirits of ancestors or the like,
nor even supposed to operate according to any human
analogy.

Up to this point Wordsworth's reminiscences may seem
simply to illustrate the conclusions which science reaches
by other roads. But he is not content with merely record-
ing and analyzing his childish impressions ; he implies, or
even asserts, that these "fancies from afar are brought"—
that the child's view of the world reveals to him truths
which the man with difficulty retains or recovers. This is
not the usual teaching of science, yet it would be hard to
assert that it is absolutely impossible. The child's instincts
may well be supposed to partake in larger measure of the
general instincts of the race, in smaller measure of the
special instincts of his own country and century, than
is the case with the man. Now the feelings and beliefs
of each successive century will probably be, on the whole,
superior to those of any previous century. But this is

not universally true; the teaching of each generation does not thus sum up the results of the whole past. And thus the child, to whom in a certain sense the past of humanity is present,—who is living through the whole life of the race in little, before he lives the life of his century in large,—may possibly dimly apprehend something more of truth in certain directions than is visible to the adults around him.

But, thus qualified, the intuitions of infancy might seem scarcely worth insisting on. And Wordsworth, as is well known, has followed Plato in advancing for the child a much bolder claim. The child's soul, in this view, has existed before it entered the body—has existed in a world superior to ours, but connected, by the immanence of the same pervading Spirit, with the material universe before our eyes. The child begins by feeling this material world strange to him. But he sees in it, as it were, what he has been accustomed to see; he discerns in it its kinship with the spiritual world which he dimly remembers; it is to him " an unsubstantial fairy place "—a scene at once brighter and more unreal than it will appear in his eyes when he has become acclimatized to earth. And even when this freshness of insight has passed away, it occasionally happens that sights or sounds of unusual beauty or carrying deep associations—a rainbow, a cuckoo's cry, a sunset of extraordinary splendour—will renew for a while this sense of vision and nearness to the spiritual world—a sense which never loses its reality, though with advancing years its presence grows briefer and more rare.

Such, then, in prosaic statement is the most characteristic message of Wordsworth. And it is to be noted that though Wordsworth at times presents it as a coherent theory, yet

it is not necessarily of the nature of a theory, nor need be
accepted or rejected as a whole; but is rather an inlet of illumining emotion in which different minds can share in the
measure of their capacities or their need.   There are some to
whom childhood brought no strange vision of brightness, but
who can feel their communion with the Divinity in Nature
growing with the growth of their souls.   There are others
who might be unwilling to acknowledge any spiritual or
transcendent source for the elevating joy which the contemplation of Nature can give, but who feel nevertheless
that to that joy Wordsworth has been their most effective
guide.   A striking illustration of this fact may be drawn
from the passage in which John Stuart Mill, a philosopher
of a very different school, has recorded the influence exercised over him by Wordsworth's poems, read in a season
of dejection, when there seemed to be no real and sub-
stantive joy in life, nothing but the excitement of the
struggle with the hardships and injustices of human fates.

" What made Wordsworth's poems a medicine for my state of
mind," he says in his Autobiography, " was that they expressed,
not mere outward beauty, but states of feeling, and of thought
coloured by feeling, under the excitement of beauty.   They
seemed to be the very culture of the feelings which I was in
quest of.   In them I seemed to draw from a source of inward
joy, of sympathetic and imaginative pleasure, which could be
shared in by all human beings, which had no connexion
with struggle or imperfection, but would be made richer by
every improvement in the physical or social condition of
mankind.   From them I seemed to learn what would be the
perennial sources of happiness, when all the greater evils of
life shall have been removed.   And I felt myself at once better
and happier as I came under their influence."

Words like these, proceeding from a mind so different
from the poet's own, form perhaps as satisfactory a testi-

mony to the value of his work as any writer can obtain. For they imply that Wordsworth has succeeded in giving his own impress to emotions which may become common to all ; that he has produced a body of thought which is felt to be both distinctive and coherent, while yet it enlarges the reader's capacities instead of making demands upon his credence. Whether there be theories, they shall pass ; whether there be systems, they shall fail ; the true epoch-maker in the history of the human soul is the man who educes from this bewildering universe a new and elevating joy.

I have alluded above to some of the passages, most of them familiar enough, in which Wordworth's sense of the mystic relation between the world without us and the world within—the correspondence between the seen and the unseen—is expressed in its most general terms. But it is evident that such a conviction as this, if it contain any truth, cannot be barren of consequences on any level of thought. The communion with Nature which is capable of being at times sublimed to an incommunicable ecstasy must be capable also of explaining Nature to us so far as she can be explained ; there must be *axiomata media* of natural religion ; there must be something in the nature of poetic truths, standing midway between mystic intuition and delicate observation.

How rich Wordsworth is in these poetic truths—how illumining is the gaze which he turns on the commonest phenomena—how subtly and variously he shows us the soul's innate perceptions or inherited memories as it were co-operating with Nature and "half creating" the voice with which she speaks—all this can be learnt by attentive study alone. Only a few scattered samples can be given here ; and I will begin with one on whose significance the poet has himself dwelt. This is the poem called *The Leech-Gatherer*, afterwards more formally named *Resolution and Independence*.

" I will explain to you," says Wordsworth, " in prose, my feelings in writing that poem. I describe myself as having been exalted to the highest pitch of delight by the joyousness and beauty of Nature ; and then as depressed, even in the midst of those beautiful objects, to the lowest dejection and despair. A young poet in the midst of the happiness of Nature is described as overwhelmed by the thoughts of the miserable reverses which have befallen the happiest of all men, viz. poets. I think of this till I am so deeply impressed with it, that I consider the manner in which I am rescued from my dejection and despair almost as an interposition of Providence. A person reading the poem with feelings like mine will have been awed and controlled, expecting something spiritual or supernatural. What is brought forward ? A lonely place, ' a pond, by which an old man *was*, far from all house or home : ' not *stood*, nor *sat*, but *was*—the figure presented in the most naked simplicity possible. The feeling of spirituality or supernaturalness is again referred to as being strong in my mind in this passage. How came he here ? thought I, or what can he be doing ? I then describe him, whether ill or well is not for me to judge with perfect confidence; but this I *can* confidently affirm, that though I believe God has given me a strong imagination, I cannot conceive a figure more impressive than that of an old man like this, the survivor of a wife and ten children, travelling alone among the mountains and all lonely places, carrying with him his own fortitude, and the necessities which an unjust state of society has laid upon him. You speak of his speech as tedious. Everything

is tedious when one does not read with the feelings of the
author.   *The Thorn* is tedious to hundreds ; and so is *The
Idiot Boy* to hundreds.   It is in the character of the old
man to tell his story, which an impatient reader must feel
tedious.   But, good heavens ! such a figure, in such a
place ;   a pious, self-respecting, miserably infirm and
pleased old man, telling such a tale ! "

The naive earnestness of this passage suggests to us how
constantly recurrent in Wordsworth'a mind were the two
trains of ideas which form the substance of the poem ;
the interaction, namely, (if so it may be termed,) of the
moods of Nature with the moods of the human mind ;
and the dignity and interest of man as man, depicted with
no complex background of social or political life, but set
amid the primary affections and sorrows, and the wild
aspects of the external world.

Among the pictures which Wordsworth has left us of
the influence of Nature on human character, *Peter Bell*
may be taken as marking one end, and the poems on *Lucy*
the other end of the scale.   Peter Bell lives in the face of
Nature untouched alike by her terror and her charm ;
Lucy's whole being is moulded by Nature's self ; she is
responsive to sun and shadow, to silence and to sound,
and melts almost into an impersonation of a Cumbrian
valley's peace.   Between these two extremes how many are
the possible shades of feeling !   In *Ruth*, for instance, the
point impressed upon us is that Nature's influence is only
salutary so long as she is herself, so to say, in keeping
with man ; that when her operations reach that degree of
habitual energy and splendour at which our love for her
passes into fascination and our admiration into bewilderment, then the fierce and irregular stimulus consorts no
longer with the growth of a temperate virtue.

> The wind, the tempest roaring high,
> The tumult of a tropic sky,
> Might well be dangerous food
> For him, a youth to whom was given
> So much of earth, so much of heaven,
> And such impetuous blood.

And a contrasting touch recalls the healing power of those gentle and familiar presences which came to Ruth in her stormy madness with visitations of momentary calm.

> Yet sometimes milder hours she knew,
> Nor wanted sun, nor rain, nor dew,
> Nor pastimes of the May;
> They all were with her in her cell;
> And a wild brook with cheerful knell
> Did o'er the pebbles play.

I will give one other instance of this subtle method of dealing with the contrasts in Nature. It is from the poem entitled "*Lines left upon a Seat in a Yew-Tree which stands near the Lake of Esthwaite, on a desolate part of the Shore, commanding a beautiful Prospect.*" This seat was once the haunt of a lonely, a disappointed, an embittered man.

> Stranger! these gloomy boughs
> Had charms for him; and here he loved to sit,
> His only visitants a straggling sheep,
> The stone-chat, or the glancing sand-piper;
> And on these barren rocks, with fern and heath
> And juniper and thistle sprinkled o'er,
> Fixing his downcast eye, he many an hour
> A morbid pleasure nourished, tracing here
> An emblem of his own unfruitful life;
> And, lifting up his head, he then would gaze
> On the more distant scene,—how lovely 'tis
> Thou seest,—and he would gaze till it became
> Far lovelier, and his heart could not contain
> The beauty, still more beauteous! Nor, that time,

When Nature had subdued him to herself,
Would he forget those beings, to whose minds,
Warm from the labours of benevolence,
The world, and human life, appeared a scene
Of kindred loveliness ; then he would sigh
With mournful joy, to think that others felt
What he must never feel : and so, lost Man !
On visionary views would fancy feed
Till his eyes streamed with tears.

This is one of the passages which the lover of Wordsworth quotes, perhaps, with some apprehension ; not
knowing how far it carries into the hearts of others its
affecting power ; how vividly it calls up before them that
mood of desolate loneliness when the whole vision of human
love and joy hangs like a mirage in the air, and only when
it seems irrecoverably distant seems also intolerably dear.
But, however, this particular passage may impress the
reader it is not hard to illustrate by abundant references
the potent originality of Wordsworth's outlook on the
external world.

There was indeed no aspect of Nature, however often
depicted, in which his seeing eye could not discern some
unnoted quality ; there was no mood to which nature
gave birth in the mind of man from which his meditation
could not disengage some element which threw light on
our inner being.   How often has the approach of evening
been described ! and how mysterious is its solemnizing
power ! Yet it was reserved for Wordsworth in his
sonnet " Hail, Twilight, sovereign of one peaceful hour,"
to draw out a characteristic of that grey waning light
which half explains to us its sombre and pervading charm.
" Day's mutable distinctions " pass away ; all in the
landscape that suggests our own age or our own handiwork
is gone ; we look on the sight seen by our remote ancestors,

and the visible present is generalized into an immeasure-
able past.

The sonnet on the Duddon beginning "What aspect
bore the Man who roved or fled First of his tribe to this
dark dell," carries back the mind along the same track,
with the added thought of Nature's permanent gentleness
amid the "hideous usages" of primeval man,—through all
which the stream's voice was innocent, and its flow benign.
"A weight of awe not easy to be borne" fell on the
poet, also, as he looked on the earliest memorials which
these remote ancestors have left us. The *Sonnet on a Stone
Circle* which opens with these words is conceived in a
strain of emotion never more needed than now,—when
Abury itself owes its preservation to the munificence
of a private individual,—when stone-circle or round-
tower, camp or dolmen, are destroyed to save a few
shillings, and occupation-roads are mended with the
immemorial altars of an unknown God. "Speak, Giant-
mother! tell it to the Morn!"—how strongly does the
heart re-echo the solemn invocation which calls on those
abiding witnesses to speak once of what they knew long
ago!

The mention of these ancient worships may lead us to
ask in what manner Wordsworth was affected by the
Nature-deities of Greece and Rome—impersonations which
have preserved through so many ages so strange a charm.
And space must be found here for the characteristic
sonnet in which the baseness and materialism of modern
life drives him back on whatsoever of illumination and
reality lay in that young ideal.

> The world is too much with us ; late and soon,
> Getting and spending, we lay waste our powers :
> Little we see in Nature that is ours ;

> We have given our hearts away, a sordid boon!
> The Sea that bares her bosom to the moon;
> The Winds that will be howling at all hours,
> And are up-gathered now like sleeping flowers;
> For this, for everything we are out of tune;
> It moves us not. Great God! I'd rather be
> A pagan suckled in a creed outworn;
> So might I, standing on this pleasant lea,
> Have glimpses that would make me less forlorn;
> Have sight of Proteus rising from the sea:
> Or hear old Triton blow his wreathèd horn.

Wordsworth's own imagination idealized Nature in a different way. The sonnet "Brook! whose society the poet seeks" places him among the men whose Nature-deities have not yet become anthropomorphic—men to whom "unknown modes of being" may seem more lovely as well as more awful than the life we know. He would not give to his idealized brook "human cheeks, channels for tears,—no Naiad shouldst thou be,"—

> It seems the Eternal Soul is clothed in thee
> With purer robes than those of flesh and blood,
> And hath bestowed on thee a better good;
> Unwearied joy, and life without its cares.

And in the *Sonnet on Calais Beach* the sea is regarded in the same way, with a sympathy (if I may so say) which needs no help from an imaginary impersonation, but strikes back to a sense of kinship which seems antecedent to the origin of man.

> It is a beauteous Evening, calm and free;
> The holy time is quiet as a Nun
> Breathless with adoration; the broad sun
> Is sinking down in its tranquillity;
> The gentleness of heaven is on the Sea:
> Listen! the mighty Being is awake,
> And doth with his eternal motion make
> A sound like thunder—everlastingly.

A comparison, made by Wordsworth himself, of his own method of observing Nature with Scott's expresses in less mystical language something of what I am endeavouring to say.

"He expatiated much to me one day," says Mr. Aubrey de Vere, "as we walked among the hills above Grasmere, on the mode in which Nature had been described by one of the most justly popular of England's modern poets—one for whom he preserved a high and affectionate respect. 'He took pains,' Wordsworth said; 'he went out with his pencil and note-book, and jotted down whatever struck him most—a river rippling over the sands, a ruined tower on a rock above it, a promontory, and a mountain-ash waving its red berries. He went home and wove the whole together into a poetical description.' After a pause, Wordsworth resumed, with a flashing eye and impassioned voice: 'But Nature does not permit an inventory to be made of her charms! He should have left his pencil and note-book at home, fixed his eye as he walked with a reverent attention on all that surrounded him, and taken all into a heart that could understand and enjoy. Then, after several days had passed by, he should have interrogated his memory as to the scene. He would have discovered that while much of what he had admired was preserved to him, much was also most wisely obliterated; that which remained—the picture surviving in his mind—would have presented the ideal and essential truth of the scene, and done so in a large part by discarding much which, though in itself striking, was not characteristic. In every scene many of the most brilliant details are but accidental; a true eye for Nature does not note them, or at least does not dwell on them.'"

How many a phrase of Wordsworth's rises in the mind in illustration of this power! phrases which embody in a single picture, or a single image,—it may be the vivid wildness of the flowery coppice, of—

Flaunting summer, when he throws
His soul into the briar-rose,—

or the melancholy stillness of the declining year,—

> Where floats
> O'er twilight fields the autumnal gossamer ;

or—as in the words which to the sensitive Charles Lamb
seemed too terrible for art—the irresponsive blankness of
the universe—

> The broad open eye of the solitary sky—

beneath which mortal hearts must make what merriment
they may.

Or take those typical stanzas in *Peter Bell*, which so long
were accounted among Wordsworth's leading absurdities.

> In vain through every changeful year
> Did Nature lead him as before ;
> A primrose by the river's brim
> A yellow primrose was to him,
> And it was nothing more.
>
> In vain, through water, earth, and air,
> The soul of happy sound was spread,
> When Peter, on some April morn,
> Beneath the broom or budding thorn,
> Made the warm earth his lazy bed.
>
> At noon, when by the forest's edge
> He lay beneath the branches high,
> The soft blue sky did never melt
> Into his heart,—he never felt
> The witchery of the soft blue sky !
>
> On a fair prospect some have looked
> And felt, as I have heard them say,
> As if the moving time had been
> A thing as steadfast as the scene
> On which they gazed themselves away.

In all these passages, it will be observed, the emotion is

educed from Nature rather than added to her; she is
treated as a mystic text to be deciphered, rather than as
a stimulus to roving imagination. This latter mood, indeed, Wordsworth feels occasionally, as in the sonnet
where the woodland sights become to him " like a dream
of the whole world ;" but it is checked by the recurring
sense that " it is our business to idealize the real, and
not to realize the ideal." Absorbed in admiration of
fantastic clouds of sunset, he feels for a moment ashamed
to think that they are unrememberable—

> They are of the sky,
> And from our earthly memory fade away.

But soon he disclaims this regret, and reasserts the paramount interest of the things that we can grasp and love.

> Grove, isle, with every shape of sky-built dome,
> Though clad in colours beautiful and pure,
> Find in the heart of man no natural home :
> The immortal Mind craves objects that endure :
> These cleave to it ; from these it cannot roam,
> Nor they from it : their fellowship is secure.

From this temper of Wordsworth's mind, it follows
that there will be many moods in which we shall not
retain him as our companion. Moods which are re-
bellious, which beat at the bars of fate ; moods of
passion reckless in its vehemence, and assuming the pri-
macy of all other emotions through the intensity of its
delight or pain ; moods of mere imaginative phantasy,
when we would fain shape from the well-worn materials
of our thought some fabric at once beautiful and new ;
from all such phases of our inward being Wordsworth
stands aloof. His poem on the nightingale and the stock-
dove illustrates with half-conscious allegory the contrast
between himself and certain other poets.

O Nightingale ! thou surely art
A creature of a fiery heart :--
These notes of thine—they pierce and pierce ;
Tumultuous harmony and fierce !
Thou sing'st as if the God of wine
Had helped thee to a Valentine ;
A song in mockery and despite
Of shades, and dews, and silent Night ;
And steady bliss, and all the loves
Now sleeping in their peaceful groves.

I heard a Stock-dove sing or say
His homely tale, this very day ;
His voice was buried among trees,
Yet to be come at by the breeze :
He did not cease ; but cooed—and cooed,
And somewhat pensively he wooed.
He sang of love with quiet blending,
Slow to begin, and never ending ;
Of serious faith and inward glee ;
That was the Song—the Song for me !

" *His voice was buried among trees*," says Wordsworth ;
" a metaphor expressing the love of *seclusion* by which
this bird is marked ; and characterizing its note as not
partaking of the shrill and the piercing, and therefore
more easily deadened by the intervening shade ; yet a
note so peculiar, and withal so pleasing, that the breeze,
gifted with that love of the sound which the poet feels,
penetrates the shade in which it is entombed, and conveys
it to the ear of the listener."

Wordsworth's poetry on the emotional side (as distinguished from its mystical or its patriotic aspects) could
hardly be more exactly described than in the above
sentence. For while there are few poems of his which
could be read to a mixed audience with the certainty of
producing an immediate impression ; yet on the other
hand all the best ones gain in an unusual degree by

repeated study; and this is especially the case with those in which some touch of tenderness is enshrined in a scene of beauty, which it seems to interpret while it is itself exalted by it. Such a poem is *Stepping Westward,* where the sense of sudden fellowship, and the quaint greeting beneath the glowing sky, seem to link man's momentary wanderings with the cosmic spectacles of heaven. Such are the lines where all the wild romance of Highland scenery, the forlornness of the solitary vales, pours itself through the lips of the maiden singing at her work, " as if her song could have no ending,"—

> Alone she cuts and binds the grain,
> And sings a melancholy strain ;
> O listen! for the Vale profound
> Is overflowing with the sound.

Such—and with how subtle a difference !—is the *Frag ment* in which a " Spirit of noonday " wears on his face the silent joy of Nature in her own recesses, undisturbed by beast, or bird, or man,—

> Nor ever was a cloudless sky
> So steady or so fair.

And such are the poems—*We are Seven, The Pet Lamb,*[1]

---

[1] The *Pet Lamb* is probably the only poem of Wordsworth's which can be charged with having done moral injury, and that to a single individual alone. "Barbara Lewthwaite," says Wordsworth, in 1843, " was not, in fact, the child whom I had seen and overheard as engaged in the poem. I chose the name for reasons implied in the above," (i. e. an account of her remarkable beauty), "and will here add a caution against the use of names of living persons. Within a few months after the publication of this poem I was much surprised, and more hurt, to find it in a child's school-book, which, having been compiled by Lindley Murray, had come into use at Grasmere School, where Barbara was a

Louisa, The Two April Mornings—in which the beauty
of rustic children melts, as it were, into Nature herself,
and the—

> Blooming girl whose hair was wet
> With points of morning dew

becomes the impersonation of the season's early joy. We
may apply, indeed, to all these girls Wordsworth's description of leverets playing on a lawn, and call them—

> Separate creatures in their several gifts
> Abounding, but so fashioned that in all
> That Nature prompts them to display, their looks,
> Their starts of motion and their fits of rest,
> An undistinguishable style appears
> And character of gladness, as if Spring
> Lodged in their innocent bosoms, and the spirit
> Of the rejoicing Morning were their own.

My limits forbid me to dwell longer on these points.
The passages which I have been citing have been for the
most part selected as illustrating the novelty and subtlety
of Wordsworth's view of Nature.   But it will now be
sufficiently clear how continually a strain of human interest is interwoven with the delight derived from impersonal things.

> Long have I loved what I behold,
> The night that calms, the day that cheers :
> The common growth of mother earth
> Suffices me—her tears, her mirth,
> Her humblest mirth and tears.

The poet of the *Waggoner*—who, himself a habitual

pupil.   And, alas, I had the mortification of hearing that she
was very vain of being thus distinguished; and in after-life she
used to say that she remembered the incident, and what I said to
her upon the occasion.''

water-drinker, has so glowingly described the glorification
which the prospect of nature receives in a half-intoxicated
brain—may justly claim that he can enter into all genuine
pleasures, even of an order which he declines for himself.
With anything that is false or artificial he cannot sympathize, nor with such faults as baseness, cruelty, rancour,
which seem contrary to human nature itself; but in dealing with faults of mere *weakness* he is far less strait-laced
than many less virtuous men.

He had, in fact, a reverence for human beings as such
which enabled him to face even their frailties without
alienation; and there was something in his own happy
exemption from such falls which touched him into regarding men less fortunate rather with pity than disdain.

> Because the unstained, the clear, the crystalline,
> Have ever in them something of benign.

His comment on Burns's *Tam o' Shanter* will perhaps
surprise some readers who are accustomed to think of him
only in his didactic attitude.

"It is the privilege of poetic genius, he says, to catch,
under certain restrictions of which perhaps at the time of
its being exerted it is but dimly conscious, a spirit of pleasure
wherever it can be found, in the walks of nature, and in the
business of men. The poet, trusting to primary instincts,
luxuriates among the felicities of love and wine, and is enraptured
while he describes the fairer aspects of war, nor does he shrink
from the company of the passion of love though immoderate—
from convivial pleasures though intemperate—nor from the
presence of war, though savage, and recognized as the handmaid
of desolation. Frequently and admirably has Burns given way
to these impulses of nature, both with reference to himself and
in describing the condition of others. Who, but some impene-

trable dunce or narrow-minded puritan in works of art, ever
read without delight the picture which he has drawn of the
convivial exaltation of the rustic adventurer Tam o' Shanter?
The poet fears not to tell the reader in the outset that his hero
was a desperate and sottish drunkard, whose excesses were as
frequent as his opportunities. This reprobate sits down to his
cups while the storm is roaring, and heaven and earth are in
confusion; the night is driven on by song and tumultuous noise,
laughter and jest thicken as the beverage improves upon the
palate—conjugal fidelity archly bends to the service of general
benevolence—selfishness is not absent, but wearing the mask of
social cordiality; and while these various elements of humanity
are blended into one proud and happy composition of elated
spirits, the anger of the tempest without doors only heightens
and sets off the enjoyment within. I pity him who cannot perceive that in all this, though there was no moral purpose, there
is a moral effect.

> Kings may be blest, but Tam was glorious,
> O'er a' the *ills* of life victorious.

What a lesson do these words convey of charitable indulgence
for the vicious habits of the principal actor in the scene, and
of those who resemble him ! Men who to the rigidly virtuous
are objects almost of loathing, and whom therefore they cannot
serve! The poet, penetrating the unsightly and disgusting
surfaces of things, has unveiled with exquisite skill the finer ties
of imagination and feeling, that often bind these beings to
practices productive of so much unhappiness to themselves, and
to those whom it is their duty to cherish ; and, as far as he puts
the reader into possession of this intelligent sympathy, he
qualifies him for exercising a salutary influence over the minds
of those who are thus deplorably enslaved."

The reverence for man as man, the sympathy for him
in his primary relations and his essential being, of which
these comments on *Tam o' Shanter* form so remarkable
an example, is a habit of thought too ingrained in all
Wordsworth's works to call for specific illustration. The

figures of *Michael*, of *Matthew*, of the *Brothers*, of the
hero of the *Excursion*, and even of the *Idiot Boy*, suggest
themselves at once in this connexion. But it should be
noted in each case how free is the poet's view from any
idealization of the poorer classes as such, from the ascrip-
tion of imaginary merits to an unknown populace which
forms the staple of so much revolutionary eloquence.
These poems, while they form the most convincing rebuke
to the exclusive pride of the rich and great, are also a
stern and strenuous incentive to the obscure and lowly.
They are pictures of the poor man's life as it is,—pictures
as free as Crabbe's from the illusion of sentiment,—but in
which the delight of mere observation (which in Crabbe
predominates) is subordinated to an intense sympathy
with all such capacities of nobleness and tenderness as
are called out by the stress and pressure of penury or
woe. They form for the folk of northern England (as
the works of Burns and Scott for the Scottish folk) a
gallery of figures that are modelled, as it were, both from
without and from within ; by one with experience so
personal as to keep every sentence vividly accurate, and
yet with an insight which could draw from that simple
life lessons to itself unknown. We may almost venture
to generalize our statement further, and to assert that no
writer since Shakespeare has left us so true a picture of
the British nation. In Milton, indeed, we have the characteristic English spirit at a whiter glow ; but it is the
spirit of the scholar only, or of the ruler, not of the
peasant, the woman, or the child. Wordsworth gives us
that spirit as it is diffused among shepherds and husbandmen,—as it exists in obscurity and at peace. And they
who know what makes the strength of nations need wish
nothing better than that the temper which he saw and

honoured among the Cumbrian dales should be the temper
of all England, now and for ever.

Our discussion of Wordsworth's form of Natural Religion
has led us back by no forced transition to the simple life
which he described and shared.   I return to the story of
his later years,—if that be called a story which derives no
interest from incident or passion, and dwells only on
the slow broodings of a meditative soul.

CHAPTER XI.

WORDSWORTH was fond of travelling, and indulged this
taste whenever he could afford it. Comparing himself
and Southey, he says in 1843 : " My lamented friend
Southey used to say that had he been a Papist, the course
of life which in all probability would have been his was
that of a Benedictine monk, in a convent furnished with
an inexhaustible library. *Books* were, in fact, his passion ;
and *wandering*, I can with truth affirm, was mine ; but
this propensity in me was happily counteracted by inability
from want of fortune to fulfil my wishes." We find
him, however, frequently able to contrive a change of
scene. His Swiss tour in 1790, his residence in France
in 1791-2, his residence in Germany, 1798-9, have been
already touched on. Then came a short visit to France
in August 1802, which produced the sonnets on Westminster Bridge and Calais Beach. The tour in Scotland
which was so fertile in poetry took place in 1803. A
second tour in Scotland, in 1814, produced the *Brownie's
Cell* and a few other pieces. And in July, 1820, he set-
out with his wife and sister and two or three other friends
for a tour through Switzerland and Italy.

This tour produced a good deal of poetry ; and here and

there are touches which recall the old inspiration. Such is the comparison of the clouds about the Engelberg to hovering angels; and such the description of the eclipse falling upon the population of statues which throng the pinnacles of Milan Cathedral. But for the most part the poems relating to this tour have an artificial look; the sentiments in the vale of Chamouni seem to have been laboriously summoned for the occasion; and the poet's admiration for the Italian maid and the Helvetian girl is a mere shadow of the old feeling for the Highland girl, to whom, in fact, he seems obliged to recur in order to give reality to his new emotion.

To conclude the subject of Wordsworth's travels, I will mention here that in 1823 he made a tour in Holland, and in 1824 in North Wales, where his sonnet to the torrent at the Devil's Bridge recalls the Swiss scenery seen in his youth with vigour and dignity. In 1828 he made another excursion in Belgium with Coleridge, and in 1829 he visited Ireland with his friend Mr. Marshall. Neither of these tours was productive. In 1831 he paid a visit with his daughter to Sir Walter Scott at Abbotsford, before his departure to seek health in Italy. Scott received them cordially, and had strength to take them to the Yarrow. " Of that excursion," says Wordsworth, " the verses *Yarrow Revisited* are a memorial. On our return in the afternoon we had to cross the Tweed, directly opposite Abbotsford. A rich, but sad light, of rather a purple than a golden hue, was spread over the Eildon hills at that moment; and, thinking it probable that it might be the last time Sir Walter would cross the stream (the Tweed), I was not a little moved, and expressed some of my feelings in the sonnet beginning, *A trouble not of clouds nor weeping rain*. At noon on Thursday we left Abbotsford, and on the morning of that day Sir Walter and I had a serious conversation, *tête-à-tête*, when he spoke with gratitude of the happy life which, upon the whole, he had led. He had written in my daughter's album, before he came into the breakfast-room that morning, a few stanzas addressed to her ; and, while putting the book into her hand, in his own study, standing by his desk, he said to her, in my presence, ' I should not have done anything of this kind but for your father's sake ; they are probably the last verses I shall ever write.' They show how much his mind was impaired : not by the strain of thought, but by the execution, some of the lines being imperfect, and one stanza wanting corresponding rhymes. One letter, the initial S., had been omitted in the spelling of his own name."

There was another tour in Scotland in 1833, which produced *Memorials* of little poetic value. And in 1837 he made a long tour in Italy with Mr. Crabb Robinson. But the poems which record this tour indicate a mind scarcely any longer susceptible to any vivid stimulus except from accustomed objects and ideas. The *Musings near Aquapendente* are musings on Scott and Helvellyn ; the *Pine Tree of Monte Mario* is interesting because Sir George Beaumont has saved it from destruction ; the *Cuckoo at Laverna* brings all childhood back into his heart. " I remember perfectly well," says Crabb Robinson, " that I heard the cuckoo at Laverna twice before he heard it ; and that it absolutely fretted him that my ear was first favoured ; and that he exclaimed with delight, ' I hear it ! I hear it !' " This was his last foreign tour ; nor, indeed, are these tours very noticeable except as showing that he was not blindly wedded to his own lake scenery ; that his admiration could face comparisons, and

keep the same vividness when he was fresh from other
orders of beauty.

The productions of these later years took for the most
part a didactic rather than a descriptive form. In the
volume entitled *Poems chiefly of Early and Later Years*,
published in 1842, were many hortatory or ecclesiastical
pieces of inferior merit, and among them various additions to the *Ecclesiastical Sketches*, a series of sonnets
begun in 1821, but which he continued to enlarge,
spending on them much of the energies of his later years.
And although it is only in a few instances—as in the
description of King's College, Cambridge—that these sonnets possess force or charm enough to rank them high as
poetry, yet they assume a certain value when we consider
not so much their own adequacy as the greater inadequacy
of all rival attempts in the same direction.

The Episcopalian Churchman, in this country or in
the United States, will certainly nowhere find presented
to him in poetical form so dignified and comprehensive a
record of the struggles and the glories, of the vicissitudes
and the edification, of the great body to which he belongs.
Next to the Anglican liturgy—though next at an immense interval—these sonnets may take rank as the
authentic exposition of her historic being—an exposition
delivered with something of her own unadorned dignity,
and in her moderate and tranquil tone.

I would not, however, seem to claim too much. The
religion which these later poems of Wordsworth's embody
is rather the stately tradition of a great Church than the
pangs and aspirations of a holy soul. There is little in
them—whether for good or evil—of the stuff of which a
Paul, a Francis, a Dominic are made. That fervent emotion—akin to the passion of love rather than to intellec-

tual or moral conviction—finds voice through singers of a
very different tone.   It is fed by an inward anguish and
felicity which, to those who have not felt them, seem as
causeless as a lover's moods ; by wrestlings not with flesh
and blood ; by nights of despairing self-abasement ; by
ecstasies of an incommunicable peace.   How great the
gulf between Wordsworth and George Herbert !—Herbert " offering at heaven, growing and groaning thither,"
—and Wordsworth, for whom the gentle regret of the
lines,—

> Me this unchartered freedom tires,
> I feel the weight of chance desires,—

forms his most characteristic expression of the self-judgment of the solitary soul.

Wordsworth accomplished one reconciliation of great
importance to mankind.   He showed, as plainly in his
way as Socrates had shown it long ago, with what readiness
a profoundly original conception of the scheme of things
will shape itself into the mould of an established and venerable faith.   He united the religion of the philosopher
with the religion of the churchman ; one rarer thing he
could not do ; he could not unite the religion of the philosopher with the religion of the saint.   It is, indeed,
evident that the most inspiring feeling which breathes
through Wordsworth's ecclesiastical pieces is not of
a doctrinal, not even of a spiritual kind.   The ecclesiastical as well as the political sentiments of his
later years are prompted mainly by the admiring love
with which he regarded the structure of English society—
seen as that society was by him in its simplest and most
poetic aspect.   This concrete attachment to the scenes
about him had always formed an important element in his
character.   Ideal politics, whether in Church or State,

had never occupied his mind, which sought rather to find
its informing principles embodied in the England of his
own day. The sonnet *On a Parsonage in Oxfordshire*
well illustrates the loving minuteness with which he
draws out the beauty and fitness of the established scheme
of things,—the power of English country life to satisfy so
many moods of feeling.

The country-seat of the English squire or nobleman has
become—may we not say?—one of the world's chosen types
of a happy and a stately home. And Wordsworth, especially in his poems which deal with Coleorton, has shown
how deeply he felt the sway of such a home's hereditary
majesty, its secure and tranquillizing charm. Yet there
are moods when the heart which deeply feels the ine-
quality of human lots turns towards a humbler ideal.
There are moments when the broad park, the halls and
towers, seem no longer the fitting frame of human greatness, but rather an isolating solitude, an unfeeling triumph
over the poor.

In such a mood of mind it will not always satisfy us to
dwell, as Wordsworth has so often done, on the virtue
and happiness that gather round a cottage hearth,—which
we must, after all, judge by a somewhat less exacting
standard. We turn rather to the "refined rusticity" of
an English Parsonage home.

> Where holy ground begins, unhallowed ends,
> Is marked by no distinguishable line ;
> The turf unites, the pathways intertwine,—

and the clergyman's abode has but so much of dignity as
befits the minister of the Church which is the hamlet's
centre ; enough to suggest the old Athenian boast of
beauty without extravagance, and study without effemi-

nacy ; enough to show that dwellings where not this
life but another is the prevailing thought and care, yet
need not lack the graces of culture, nor the loves of
home.

The sonnet on *Seathwaite Chapel*, and the life of
Robert Walker, the incumbent of Seathwaite, which is
given at length in the notes to the sonnets on the
Duddon, afford a still more characteristic instance of the
clerical ideal towards which Wordsworth naturally
turned. In Robert Walker he had a Cumbrian statesman
turned into a practical saint ; and he describes him with a
gusto in which his laboured sonnets on *Laud* or on *Dissen-
sions* are wholly deficient.

It was in social and political matters that the consequences of this idealizing view of the facts around him
in Cumberland were most apparent. Take education, for
example. Wordsworth, as has been already stated, was
one of the earliest and most impressive assertors of the
national duty of teaching every English child to read.
He insists on this with a prosaic earnestness which places
several pages of the *Excursion* among what may be called
the standing bugbears which his poems offer to the inex-
perienced reader. And yet as soon as, through the
exertions of Bell and Lancaster, there seems to be some
chance of really educating the poor, Dr. Bell, whom
Coleridge fondly imagines as surrounded in heaven by
multitudes of grateful angels, is to Wordsworth a name of
horror. The mistresses trained on his system are called
" Dr. Bell's sour-looking teachers in petticoats." And the
instruction received in these new-fangled schools is compared to " the training that fits a boxer for victory in the
ring." The reason of this apparent inconsistency is not
far to seek. Wordsworth's eyes were fixed on the village

life around. him. Observation of that life impressed on
him the imperative necessity of instruction in reading.
But it was from a moral, rather than an intellectual
point of view that he regarded it as needful, and, this
opening into the world of ideas once secured, he held that
the cultivation of the home affections and home duties
was all that was needed beyond. And thus the Westmoreland dame, "in her summer seat in the garden, and
in winter by the fireside," was elevated into the unexpected
position of the ideal instructress of youth.

Conservatism of this kind could provoke nothing but a
sympathetic smile. The case was different when the same
conservative—even retrograde—tendency showed itself on
subjects on which party-feeling ran high. A great part of
the meditative energy of Wordsworth's later years was
absorbed by questions towards whose solution he contri-
buted no new element, and which filled him with dispro-
portionate fears. And some injustice has been done to
his memory by those who have not fully realized the pre-
disposing causes which were at work,—the timidity of age,
and the deep-rooted attachment to the England which he
knew.

I speak of age, perhaps, somewhat prematurely, as the
poet's gradually growing conservatism culminated in his
opposition to the Catholic Relief Bill, before he was sixty
years old. But there is nothing to wonder at in the fact
that the mind of a man of brooding and solitary habits
should show traces of advancing age earlier than is the
case with statesmen or men of the world, who are obliged
to keep themselves constantly alive to the ideas of the
generation that is rising around them. A deadness to
new impressions, an unwillingness to make intellectual
efforts in fresh directions, a tendency to travel the same

M

mental pathways over and over again, and to wear the
ruts of prejudice deeper at every step; such traces of age
as these undoubtedly manifested themselves in the way in
which the poet confronted the great series of changes—
Catholic Emancipation, Reform Bill, New Poor Law, on
which England entered about the year 1829. "My sixty-
second year," Wordsworth writes, in 1832, "will soon be
completed; and though I have been favoured thus far in
health and strength beyond most men of my age, yet I
feel its effects upon my spirits; they sink under a pressure of apprehension to which, at an earlier period of my
life, they would probably have been superior." To this
it must be added, that the increasing weakness of the
poet's eyes seriously limited his means of information.
He had never read much contemporary literature, and he
read less than ever now. He had no fresh or comprehensive knowledge of the general condition of the country,
and he really believed in the prognostication which was
uttered by many also who did *not* believe in it, that with
the Reform Bill the England which he knew and loved
would practically disappear. But there was nothing in
him of the angry polemic, nothing of the calumnious
partisan. One of the houses where Mr. Wordsworth was
most intimate and most welcome was that of a reforming
member of parliament, who was also a manufacturer, thus
belonging to the two classes for which the poet had the
greatest abhorrence. But the intimacy was never for a
moment shaken, and indeed in that house Mr. Wordsworth
expounded the ruinous tendency of Reform and manufac-
tures with even unusual copiousness, on account of the admiring affection with which he felt himself surrounded. The
tone in which he spoke was never such as could give pain
or excite antagonism; and—if I may be pardoned for descend-

ing to a detail which well illustrates my position—the only
rejoinder which these diatribes provoked was that the poet
on his arrival was sometimes decoyed into uttering them to
the younger members of the family, whose time was of less
value, so as to set his mind free to return to those topics of
more permanent interest where his conversation kept to the
last all that tenderness, nobility, wisdom, which in that
family, as in many others familiar with the celebrated
persons of that day, won for him a regard and a reverence
such as was accorded to no other man.

To those, indeed, who realized how deeply he felt these
changes,—how profoundly his notion of national happiness
was bound up with a lovely and vanishing ideal,—the
prominent reflection was that the hopes and principles
which maintained through all an underlying hope and
trust in the future must have been potent indeed. It was
no easy optimism which prompted the lines written in
1837—one of his latest utterances—in which he speaks to
himself with strong self-judgment and resolute hope. On
reading them one shrinks from dwelling longer upon an
old man's weakness and a brave man's fears.

> If this great world of joy and pain
>   Revolve in one sure track;
> If Freedom, set, revive again,
>   And Virtue, flown, come back,—
>
> Woe to the purblind crew who fill
>   The heart with each day's care,
> Nor learn, from past and future, skill
>   To bear and to forbear.

The poet had also during these years more of private
sorrow than his tranquil life had for a long time experienced. In 1832 his sister had a most serious illness,

which kept her for many months in a state of great prostration, and left her, when the physical symptoms abated, with her intellect painfully impaired, and her bright nature permanently overclouded. Coleridge, too, was nearing his end. " He and my beloved sister," writes Wordsworth, in 1832, "are the two beings to whom my intellect is most indebted, and they are now proceeding, as it were, *pari passu*, along the path of sickness, I will not say towards the grave, but I trust towards a blessed immortality."

In July, 1834, " every mortal power of Coleridge was frozen at its marvellous source." And although the early intimacy had scarcely been maintained,—though the "comfortless and hidden well" had, for a time at least, replaced the " living murmuring fount of love " which used to spring beside Wordsworth's door,—yet the loss was one which the surviving poet deeply felt. Coleridge was the only contemporary man of letters with whom Wordsworth's connexion had been really close ; and when Wordsworth is spoken of as one of a group of poets exemplifying in various ways the influence of the Revolution, it is not always remembered how very little he had to do with the other famous men of his time. Scott and Southey were valued friends, but he thought little of Scott's poetry, and less of Southey's. Byron and Shelley he seems scarcely to have read ; and there is nothing to show that he had ever heard of Keats. But to Coleridge his mind constantly reverted ; he called him "the most wonderful man he had ever known," and he kept him as the ideal auditor of his own poems, long after Coleridge had listened to the *Prelude*,—

A song divine of high and passionate thoughts
To their own music chanted.

In 1836, moreover, died one for whom Coleridge, as
well as Wordsworth, had felt a very high respect and regard—Sarah Hutchinson, Mrs. Wordsworth's sister, and long
the inmate of Wordsworth's household. This most valued
friend had been another instance of the singular good
fortune which attended Wordsworth in his domestic connexions; and when she was laid in Grasmere churchyard,
the stone above her tomb expressed the wish of the poet
and his wife that, even as her remains were laid beside
their dead children's, so their own bodies also might be
laid by hers.

And now, while the inner circle of friends and relations
began to pass away, the outer circle of admirers was
rapidly spreading. Between the years 1830 and 1840
Wordsworth passed from the apostle of a clique into the
most illustrious man of letters in England. The rapi-
dity of this change was not due to any remarkable
accident, nor to the appearance of any new work of
genius. It was merely an extreme instance of what must
always occur where an author, running counter to the
fashion of his age, has to create his own public in
defiance of the established critical powers. The disciples
whom he draws round him are for the most part young;
the established authorities are for the most part old; so
that by the time that the original poet is about sixty years
old, most of his admirers will be about forty, and most of
his critics will be dead. His admirers now become his
accredited critics; his works are widely introduced to the
public; and if they are really good his reputation is
secure. In Wordsworth's case the detractors had been
unusually persistent, and the reaction, when it came, was
therefore unusually violent; it was even somewhat facti-
tious in its extent; and the poems were forced by

enthusiasts upon a public which was only half ripe for
them. After the poet's death a temporary counter-reaction
succeeded, and his fame is only now finding its permanent
level.

Among the indications of growing popularity was the
publication of an American edition of Wordsworth's
poems in 1837, by Professor Reed of Philadelphia, with
whom the poet interchanged many letters of interest.
" The acknowledgments," he says in one of these, " which
I receive from the vast continent of America are among
the most grateful that reach me. What a vast field is
there open to the English mind, acting through our noble
language ! Let us hope that our authors of true genius
will not be unconscious of that thought, or inattentive to
the duty which it imposes upon them, of doing their
utmost to instruct, to purify, and to elevate their
readers."

But of all the manifestations of the growing honour in
which Wordsworth was held, none was more marked or
welcome than the honorary degree of D.C.L. conferred on
him by the University of Oxford in the summer of 1839.
Keble, as Professor of Poetry, introduced him in words of
admiring reverence, and the enthusiasm of the audience
was such as had never been evoked in that place before,
" except upon the occasions of the visits of the Duke of
Wellington." The collocation was an interesting one. The
special claim advanced for Wordsworth by Keble in his
Latin oration was " that he had shed a celestial light upon
the affections, the occupations, the piety of the poor." And
to many men besides the author of the *Christian Year* it
seemed that this striking scene was, as it were, another
visible triumph of the temper of mind which is of the
essence of Christianity ; a recognition that one spirit

more had become as a little child, and had entered into
the kingdom of heaven.

In October, 1842, another token of public respect was
bestowed on him in the shape of an annuity of 300*l.* a
year from the Civil List for distinguished literary merit.
"I need scarcely add," says Sir Robert Peel, in making
the offer, "that the acceptance by you of this mark of
favour from the Crown, considering the grounds on which
it is proposed, will impose no restraint upon your perfect
independence, and involve no obligation of a personal
nature." In March, 1843, came the death of Southey, and
in a few days Wordsworth received a letter from Earl De
la Warr, the Lord Chamberlain, offering him, in the most
courteous terms, the office of Poet Laureate, which, however, he respectfully declined as imposing duties, "which,
far advanced in life as I am, I cannot venture to undertake."

This letter brought a reply from the Lord Chamberlain,
pressing the office on him again, and a letter from Sir
Robert Peel which gave dignified expression to the
national feeling in the matter. "The offer," he says,
"was made to you by the Lord Chamberlain, with my
entire concurrence, not for the purpose of imposing on
you any onerous or disagreeable duties, but in order to
pay you that tribute of respect which is justly due to the
first of living poets. The Queen entirely approved of the
nomination, and there is one unanimous feeling on the
part of all who have heard of the proposal (and it is
pretty generally known) that there could not be a question
about the selection. Do not be deterred by the fear of
any obligations which the appointment may be supposed
to imply. I will undertake that you shall have nothing
required from you. But as the Queen can select for this

honourable appointment no one whose claims for respect
and honour, on account of eminence as a poet, can be
placed in competition with yours, · I trust you will not
longer hesitate to accept it."

This letter overcame the aged poet's scruples; and he
filled with silent dignity the post of Laureate till after
seven years' space a worthy successor received

> This laurel greener from the brows
> Of him that uttered nothing base.

CHAPTER XII.

WORDSWORTH'S appointment to the Laureateship was
significant in more ways than one. He was so much
besides a poet, that his appointment implied something of
a national recognition, not only of his past poetical
achievements, but of the substantial truth of that body
of principles which through many years of neglect and
ridicule he had consistently supported. There was therefore nothing incongruous in the fact that the only
composition of any importance which Wordsworth produced after he became Laureate was in prose—his two
letters on the projected Kendal and Windermere railway, 1844. No topic, in fact, could have arisen on
which the veteran poet could more fitly speak with whatever authority his official spokesmanship of the nation's
higher life could give, for it was a topic with every aspect
of which he was familiar; and so far as the extension of
railways through the Lake country was defended on
grounds of popular benefit, (and not merely of commercial
advantage), no one, certainly, had shown himself more
capable of estimating at their full value such benefits as
were here proposed.

The results which follow on a large incursion of visitors

into the Lake country may be considered under two heads,
as affecting the residents, or as affecting the visitors themselves. And first as to the residents. Of the wealthier
class of these I say nothing, as it will perhaps be thought
that their inconvenience is outweighed by the possible
profits which the railway may bring to speculators or
contractors. But the effect produced on the poorer
residents,—on the peasantry,—is a serious matter, and the
danger which was distantly foreseen by Wordsworth has
since his day assumed grave proportions. And lest the
poet's estimate of the simple virtue which is thus jeo-
pardized should be suspected of partiality, it may be
allowable to corroborate it by the testimony of an eminent
man, not a native of the district, though a settler therein
in later life, and whose writings, perhaps, have done more
than any man's since Wordsworth to increase the sum
of human enjoyment derived both from Art and from
Nature.

"The Border peasantry of Scotland and England," says
Mr. Ruskin,[1] "painted with absolute fidelity by Scott and
Wordsworth,—(for leading types out of this exhaustless
portraiture, I may name Dandie Dinmont, and Michael,)
are hitherto a scarcely injured race ; whose strength and
virtue yet survive to represent the body and soul of
England, before her days of mechanical decrepitude, and
commercial dishonour. There are men working in my
own fields who might have fought with Henry the Fifth
at Agincourt, without being discerned from among his
knights ; I can take my tradesmen's word for a thousand
pounds ; my garden gate opens on the latch to the public
road, by day and night, without fear of any foot entering

---

[1] *A Protest against the Extension of Railways in the Lake District.*—Simpkin, Marshall, and Co., 1876.

but my own ; and my girl-guests may wander by road or moorland, or through every bosky dell of this wild wood, free as the heather-bees or squirrels. What effect on the character of such a population will be produced by the influx of that of the suburbs of our manufacturing towns there is evidence enough, if the reader cares to ascertain the facts, in every newspaper on his morning table."

There remains the question of how the greatest benefit is to be secured to visitors to the country, quite apart from the welfare of its more permanent inhabitants. At first sight this question seems to present a problem of a well-known order—to find the point of maximum pleasure to mankind in a case where the intensity of the pleasure varies inversely as its extension—where each fresh person who shares it diminishes *pro tanto* the pleasure of the rest. But, as Wordsworth has pointed out, this is not in reality the question here. To the great mass of cheap excursionists the characteristic scenery of the Lakes is in itself hardly a pleasure at all. The pleasure, indeed, which they derive from contact with Nature is great and important, but it is one which could be offered to them, not only as well but much better, near their own homes.

" It is benignly ordained that green fields, clear blue skies, running streams of pure water, rich groves and woods, orchards, and all the ordinary varieties of rural nature should find an easy way to the affections of all men. But a taste beyond this, however desirable it may be that every one should possess it, is not to be implanted at once ; it must be gradually developed both in nations and individuals. Rocks and mountains, torrents and wide-spread waters, and all those features of nature which go to the composition of such scenes as this part of England is distinguished for, cannot, in their finer relations to the human mind, be comprehended, or even very

imperfectly conceived, without processes of culture or opportunities of observation in some degree habitual.   In the eye of
thousands, and tens of thousands, a rich meadow, with fat cattle
grazing upon it, or the sight of what they would call a heavy
crop of corn, is worth all that the Alps and Pyrenees in their
utmost grandeur and beauty could show to them ; and it is
noticeable what trifling conventional prepossessions will, in
common minds, not only preclude pleasure from the sight of
natural beauty, but will even turn it into an object of disgust.
In the midst of a small pleasure-ground immediately below my
house, rises a detached rock, equally remarkable for the beauty
of its form, the ancient oaks that grow out of it, and the flowers
and shrubs which adorn it.   ' What a nice place would this be,'
said a Manchester tradesman, pointing to the rock, ' if that ugly
lump were but out of the way.'   Men as little advanced in the
pleasure which such objects give to others, are so far from being
rare that they may be said fairly to represent a large majority
of mankind.   This is the fact, and none but the deceiver and
the willingly deceived can be offended by its being stated."

And, since this is so, the true means of raising the
taste of the masses consists, as Wordsworth proceeds to
point out, in giving them,—not a few hurried glimpses of
what is above their comprehension,—but permanent opportunities of learning at leisure the first great lessons which
Nature has to teach.   Since he wrote thus our towns have
spread their blackness wider still, and the provision of
parks for the recreation of our urban population has
become a pressing national need.   And here again the
very word *recreation* suggests another unfitness in the
Lake country for these purposes.   Solitude is as characteristic of that region as beauty, and what the mass of
mankind need for their refreshment—most naturally and
justly—is not solitude but society.

> The silence that is in the starry sky,
> The sleep that is among the lonely hills,

is to them merely a drawback, to be overcome by moving
about in large masses, and by congregating in chosen
resorts with vehement hilarity. It would be most unreasonable to wish to curtail the social expansion of men
whose lives are for the most part passed in a monotonous
round of toil. But is it kinder and wiser,—from any
point of view but the railway shareholder's,—to allure
them into excursion trains by the prestige of a scenery
which is to them (as it was to all classes a century or two
ago) at best indifferent, or to provide them near at hand
with their needed space for rest and play, not separated
from their homes by hours of clamour and crowding, nor
broken up by barren precipices, nor drenched with
sweeping storm?

Unquestionably it is the masses whom we have first to
consider. Sooner than that the great mass of the dwellers
in towns should be debarred from the influences of Nature
—sooner than that they should continue for another century to be debarred as now they are—it might be better
that Cumbrian statesmen and shepherds should be turned
into innkeepers and touts, and that every poet, artist,
dreamer, in England should be driven to seek his
solitude at the North Pole. But it is the mere futility
of sentiment to pretend that there need be any real col-
lision of interests here. There is space enough in England
yet for all to enjoy in their several manners, if those who
have the power would leave some unpolluted rivers, and
some unblighted fields, for the health and happiness of
the factory-hand, whose toil is for their fortunes, and
whose degradation is their shame.

Wordsworth, while indicating, with some such reasoning as this, the true method of promoting the education
of the mass of men in natural joys, was assuredly not

likely to forget that in every class, even the poorest, are
found exceptional spirits which some inbred power has
attuned already to the stillness and glory of the hills. In
what way the interests of such men may best be consulted,
he has discussed in the following passage.

> " O nature, a' thy shows an' forms
> To feeling pensive hearts hae charms !"

" So exclaimed the Ayrshire ploughman, speaking of
ordinary rural nature under the varying influences of the
seasons; and the sentiment has found an echo in the
bosoms of thousands in as humble a condition as he himself was when he gave vent to it. But then they *were*
feeling, pensive hearts—men who would be among the
first to lament the facility with which they had approached
this region, by a sacrifice of so much of its quiet and
beauty as, from the intrusion of a railway, would be
inseparable. What can, in truth, be more absurd than
that either rich or poor should be spared the trouble of
travelling by the high roads over so short a space, according to their respective means, if the unavoidable consequence must be a great disturbance of the retirement, and,
in many places, a destruction of the beauty, of the country
which the parties are come in search of? Would not this
be pretty much like the child's cutting up his drum to
learn where the sound came from?"

The truth of these words has become more conspicuous
since Wordsworth's day. The Lake country is now both
engirdled and intersected with railways. The point to
which even the poorest of genuine lovers of the mountains
could desire that his facilities of cheap locomotion should
be carried has been not only reached but far overpassed.
If he is not content to dismount from his railway car-

riage at Coniston, or Seascale, or Bowness,—at Penrith, or
Troutbeck, or Keswick,— and to move at eight miles an
hour in a coach, or at four miles an hour on foot, while
he studies that small intervening tract of country, of
which every mile is a separate gem,—when, we may ask,
is he to dismount? what *is* he to study? Or is nothing
to be expected from Nature but a series of dissolving
views?

It is impossible to feel sanguine as to the future of this
irreplaceable national possession. A real delight in scenery,
—apart from the excitements of sport or mountaineering,
for which Scotland and Switzerland are better suited than
Cumberland,—is still too rare a thing among the wealthier
as among the poorer classes to be able to compete with
such a power as the Railway Interest. And it is little
likely now that the Government of England should act
with regard to this district as the Government of the
United States has acted with regard to the Yosemite and
Yellowstone valleys, and guard as a national possession
the beauty which will become rarer and more precious
with every generation of men. But it is in any case
desirable that Wordsworth's unanswered train of reasoning
on the subject should be kept in view—that it should be
clearly understood that the one argument for making more
railways through the Lakes is that they may possibly pay;
while it is certain that each railway extension is injurious
to the peasantry of the district, and to all visitors who
really care for its scenery, while conferring no benefit on
the crowds who are dragged many miles to what they do
not enjoy, instead of having what they really want
secured to them, as it ought to be, at their own doors.

It is probable that all this will continue to be said in
vain. Railways, and mines, and waterworks will have

their way, till injury has become destruction. The
natural sanctuary of England, the nurse of simple and
noble natures, "the last region which Astræa touches with
flying feet," will be sacrificed—it is scarcely possible to
doubt it—to the greed of gain. We must seek our con-
solation in the thought that no outrage on Nature is
mortal; that the ever-springing affections of men create
for themselves continually some fresh abode, and inspire
some new landscape with a consecrating history, and as
it were with a silent soul. Yet it will be long ere round
some other lakes, upon some other hill, shall cluster
memories as pure and high as those which hover still
around Rydal and Grasmere, and on Helvellyn's windy
summit, "and by Glenridding Screes and low Glencoign."

With this last word of protest and warning,—uttered,
as it may seem to the reader, with unexpected force and
conviction from out of the tranquillity of a serene old
age,—Wordsworth's mission is concluded. The prophecy
of his boyhood is fulfilled, and the "dear native regions"
whence his dawning genius rose have been gilded by the
last ray of its declining fire. There remains but the
domestic chronicle of a few more years of mingled sadness and peace. And I will first cite a characteristic passage from a letter to his American correspondent, Mr.
Reed, describing his presentation as Laureate to the
Queen :—

"The reception given me by the Queen at her ball was
most gracious. Mrs. Everett, the wife of your Minister,
among many others, was a witness to it, without knowing
who I was. It moved her to the shedding of tears.
This effect was in part produced, I suppose, by American
habits of feeling, as pertaining to a republican government. To see a grey-haired man of seventy-five years of

age, kneeling down in a large assembly to kiss the hand of a young woman, is a sight for which institutions essentially democratic do not prepare a spectator of either sex, and must naturally place the opinions upon which a republic is founded, and the sentiments which support it, in strong contrast with a government based and upheld as ours is."

In the same letter the poet introduces an ominous allusion to the state of his daughter's health. Dora, his only daughter who survived childhood, was the darling of Wordsworth's age. In her wayward gaiety and bright intelligence there was much to remind him of his sister's youth; and his clinging nature wound itself round this new Dora as tenderly as it had ever done round her who was now only the object of loving compassion and care. In 1841 Dora Wordsworth married Mr. Quillinan, an ex-officer of the Guards, and a man of great literary taste and some original power. In 1821 he had settled for a time in the vale of Rydal, mainly for the sake of Wordsworth's society; and ever since then he had been an intimate and valued friend. He had been married before, but his wife died in 1822, leaving him two daughters, one of whom was named from the murmuring Rotha, and was god-child of the poet. Shortly after marriage, Dora Quillinan's health began to fail. In 1845 the Quillinans went to Oporto in search of health, and returned in 1846, in the trust that it was regained. But in July 1847 Dora Quillinan died at Rydal, and left her father to mourn for his few remaining years his "immeasurable loss."

The depth and duration of Wordsworth's grief in such bereavements as fell to his lot, was such as to make his friends thankful that his life had on the whole been guided through ways of so profound a peace.

Greatly, indeed, have they erred, who have imagined him as cold, or even as by nature tranquil. "What strange workings," writes one from Rydal Mount when the poet was in his sixty-ninth year,—"what strange workings are there in his great mind! How fearfully strong are all his feelings and affections! If his intellect had been less powerful they must have destroyed him long ago." Such, in fact, was the impression which he gave to those who knew him best throughout life. The look of premature age, which De Quincey insists on ; the furrowed and rugged countenance, the brooding intensity of the eye, the bursts of anger at the report of evil doings, the lonely and violent roamings over the mountains,—all told of a strong absorption and a smothered fire. His own description of himself, in his *Imitation of the Castle of Indolence,* unexpected as it is by the ordinary reader, carries for those who knew him the stamp of truth.

> Full many a time, upon a stormy night,
> His voice came to us from the neighbouring height :
> Oft did we see him driving full in view
> At mid-day when the sun was shining bright;
> What ill was on him, what he had to do,
> A mighty wonder bred among our quiet crew.

> Ah ! piteous sight it was to see this Man
> When he came back to us, a withered flower,—
> Or like a sinful creature, pale and wan.
> Down would he sit ; and without strength or power
> Look at the common grass from hour to hour :
> And oftentimes, how long I fear to say,
> Where apple-trees in blossom made a bower,
> Retired in that sunshiny shade he lay ;
> And, like a naked Indian, slept himself away.

Great wonder to our gentle tribe it was
Whenever from our valley he withdrew ;
For happier soul no living creature has
Than he had, being here the long day thr ough.
Some thought he was a lover, and did woo :
Some thought far worse of him, and judged him wrong :
But Verse was what he had been wedded to ;
And his own mind did like a tempest strong
Come to him thus, and drove the weary wight along.

An excitement which vents itself in bodily exercise
carries its own sedative with it. And in comparing
Wordsworth's nature with that of other poets whose
career has been less placid, we may say that he was
perhaps not less excitable than they, but that it was his
constant endeavour to avoid all excitement, save of the
purely poetic kind ; and that the outward circumstances of
his life,—his mediocrity of fortune, happy and early
marriage, and absence of striking personal charm,—made it
easy for him to adhere to a method of life which was, in the
truest sense of the term, *stoic*—stoic alike in its practical
abstinences and in its calm and grave ideal. Purely poetic
excitement, however, is hard to maintain at a high point ;
and the description quoted above of the voice which came
through the stormy night should be followed by another
—by the same candid and self-picturing hand—which
represents the same habits in a quieter light.

"Nine-tenths of my verses," says the poet in 1843,
"have been murmured out in the open air. One day a
stranger, having walked round the garden and grounds of
Rydal Mount, asked of one of the female servants, who
happened to be at the door, permission to see her master's
study. 'This,' said she, leading him forward, 'is my
master's library, where he keeps his books, but his study
is out of doors.' After a long absence from home, it has

more than once happened that some one of my cottage neighbours (not of the double-coach-house cottages) has said, 'Well, there he is! we are glad to hear him *booing* about again.'"

Wordsworth's health, steady and robust for the most part, indicated the same restrained excitability. While he was well able to resist fatigue, exposure to weather, &c. there were, in fact, three things which his peculiar constitution made it difficult for him to do, and unfortunately those three things were reading, writing, and the composition of poetry. A frequently recurring inflammation of the eyes, caught originally from exposure to a cold wind when overheated by exercise, but always much aggravated by mental excitement, sometimes prevented his reading for months together. His symptoms when he attempted to hold the pen are thus described, in a published letter to Sir George Beaumont (1803):—

"I do not know from what cause it is, but during the last three years I have never had a pen in my hand for five minutes before my whole frame becomes a bundle of uneasiness; a perspiration starts out all over me, and my chest is oppressed in a manner which I cannot describe." While as to the labour of composition his sister says (September 1800): "He writes with so much feeling and agitation that it brings on a sense of pain and internal weakness about his left side and stomach, which now often makes it impossible for him to write when he is, in mind and feelings, in such a state that he could do it without difficulty."

But turning to the brighter side of things—to the joys rather than the pains of the sensitive body and spirit—we find in Wordsworth's later years much of happiness on which to dwell. The memories which his name recalls

are for the most part of thoughtful kindnesses, of simple-
hearted joy in feeling himself at last appreciated, of tender
sympathy with the young.   Sometimes it is a recollection
of some London drawing-room, where youth and beauty
surrounded the rugged old man with an eager admiration
which fell on no unwilling heart.   Sometimes it is a story
of some assemblage of young and old, rich and poor, from
all the neighbouring houses and cottages, at Rydal Mount,
to keep the aged poet's birthday with a simple feast and
rustic play.   Sometimes it is a report of some fireside
gathering at Lancrigg or Foxhow, where the old man
grew eloquent as he talked of Burns and Coleridge, of
Homer and Virgil, of the true aim of poetry and the true
happiness of man.   Or we are told of some last excursion
to well-loved scenes ; of holly-trees planted by the poet's
hands to stimulate nature's decoration on the craggy
hill.

Such are the memories of those who best remember him.
To those who were young children while his last years
went by he seemed a kind of mystical embodiment of the
lakes and mountains round him—a presence without which
they would not be what they were.   And now he is gone,
and their untouched and early charm is going too.

> Heu, tua nobis
> Pæne simul tecum solatia rapta, Menalca !

Rydal Mount, of which he had at one time feared to be
deprived, was his to the end.   He still paced the terrace-
walks—but now the flat terrace oftener than the sloping
one—whence the eye travels to lake and mountain across
a tossing gulf of green.   The doves that so long had been
wont to answer with murmurs of their own to his "half-
formed melodies " still hung in the trees above his path-

way; and many who saw him there must have thought of
the lines in which his favourite poet congratulates himself
that he has not been exiled from his home.

> Calm as thy sacred streams thy years shall flow ;
> Groves which thy youth has known thine age shall know ;
> Here, as of old, Hyblæan bees shall twine
> Their mazy murmur into dreams of thine,—
> Still from the hedge's willow-bloom shall come
> Through summer silences a slumberous hum,—
> Still from the crag shall lingering winds prolong
> The half-heard cadence of the woodman's song,—
> While evermore the doves, thy love and care,
> Fill the tall elms with sighing in the air.

Yet words like these fail to give the solemnity of his
last years,—the sense of grave retrospection, of humble
self-judgment, of hopeful looking to the end. "It is
indeed a deep satisfaction," he writes near the close of
life, "to hope and believe that my poetry will be while it
lasts, a help to the cause of virtue and truth, especially
among the young. As for myself, it seems now of little
moment how long I may be remembered. When a man
pushes off in his little boat into the great seas of Infinity
and Eternity, it surely signifies little how long he is kept
in sight by watchers from the shore."

And again, to an intimate friend, "Worldly-minded I
am not ; on the contrary, my wish to benefit those within
my humble sphere strengthens seemingly in exact proportion to my inability to realize those wishes. What I lament
most is that the spirituality of my nature does not expand
and rise the nearer I approach the grave, as yours does,
and as it fares with my beloved partner."

The aged poet might feel the loss of some vividness of
emotion, but his thoughts dwelt more and more constantly
on the unseen world. One of the images which recurs

oftenest to his friends is that of the old man as he would
stand against the window of the dining-room at Rydal
Mount and read the Psalms and Lessons for the day; of
the tall bowed figure and the silvery hair; of the deep
voice which always faltered when among the prayers he
came to the words which give thanks for those "who have
departed this life in Thy faith and fear."

There is no need to prolong the narration. As healthy
infancy is the same for all, so the old age of all good men
brings philosopher and peasant once more together, to meet
with the same thoughts the inevitable hour. Whatever
the well-fought fight may have been, rest is the same for
all.

> Retirement then might hourly look
>   Upon a soothing scene ;
> Age steal to his allotted nook
>   Contented and serene ;
> With heart as calm as lakes that sleep,
>   In frosty moonlight glistening,
> Or mountain torrents, where they creep
> Along a channel smooth and deep,
>   To their own far-off murmurs listening.

What touch has given to these lines their impress of an
unfathomable peace ? For there speaks from them a tranquillity which seems to overcome our souls ; which makes
us feel in the midst of toil and passion that we are dis-
quieting ourselves in vain ; that we are travelling to a
region where these things shall not be ; that "so shall
immoderate fear leave us, and inordinate love shall die."

Wordsworth's last days were absolutely tranquil. A
cold caught on a Sunday afternoon walk brought on a
pleurisy. He lay for some weeks in a state of passive
weakness ; and at last Mrs. Wordsworth said to him,
"William, you are going to Dora." "He made no reply at

the time, and the words seem to have passed unheeded; indeed, it was not certain that they had been even heard. More than twenty-four hours afterwards one of his nieces came into his room, and was drawing aside the curtain of his chamber, and then, as if awakening from a quiet sleep, he said, ' Is that Dora ? ' "

On Tuesday, April 23, 1850, as his favourite cuckoo-clock struck the hour of noon, his spirit passed away. His body was buried, as he had wished, in Grasmere churchyard. Around him the dalesmen of Grasmere lie beneath the shade of sycamore and yew; and Rotha's murmur mourns the pausing of that " music sweeter than her own." And surely of him, if of any one, we may think as of a man who was so in accord with Nature, so at one with the very soul of things, that there can be no Mansion of the Universe which shall not be to him a home, no Governor who will not accept him among His servants, and satisfy him with love and peace.

THE END.

GILBERT AND RIVINGTON, PRINTERS, ST. JOHN'S SQUARE, E.C.

For EU product safety concerns, contact us at Calle de José Abascal, 56–1°,
28003 Madrid, Spain or eugpsr@cambridge.org.

www.ingramcontent.com/pod-product-compliance
Ingram Content Group UK Ltd.
Pitfield, Milton Keynes, MK11 3LW, UK
UKHW012344130625
459647UK00009B/524